Evolution
Colin Patterson

British Museum (Natural History)
London

© Trustees of the British Museum (Natural History) 1978
Publication number 783
ISBN 0 565 00783 1
Printed in England by Butler & Tanner Ltd, Frome and London

Contents

Foreword

In writing this book I have set out to produce an account of modern evolutionary theory which does not beg too many questions, and is complete enough to be coherent, but simple enough to be comprehensible to those with little or no technical knowledge of biology. The book may not be easy reading for such people, mainly because an understanding of evolution requires a knowledge of genetics, which is not an easy subject. Nevertheless, I hope that the subject is important enough for the effort to be worthwhile. I have found it impossible to avoid using technical words, except by clumsy circumlocutions that would make the book much longer. But I have used as few as possible, tried to define each one the first time it is used, and there is a glossary at the end.

If readers find some passages particularly obscure, long-winded or over-simplified, I would be glad to hear from them, so that I can try to cure the defects.

1 Propositions

The modern theory of evolution is the basis of biological science. It is an idea that unifies and directs work in all sorts of specialized fields, from medicine to geology. This theory is often called neo-Darwinian: 'Darwinian' because it uses Darwin's idea of natural selection, and 'neo' (new) because it incorporates a theory of heredity, worked out since Darwin's time. The theory can be summarized in five propositions:

Reproduction 'Like begets like': reproduction in populations of organisms produces descendent populations of similar organisms.

Excess The reproductive potential of the parent population always greatly exceeds the actual number of its descendants.

Variation Members of a population always vary; much of this variation is transmitted to the descendants (heritable), and novelties (mutations) may appear.

Environmental selection The space and resources of the environment are limited, so that there is competition within and between populations. Individuals possessing favourable characteristics, of whatever sort, will tend to compete successfully and leave more descendants than other, less favourably endowed individuals.

Divergence The environment varies with time and from place to place. Heritable variations which suit a particular environment will be selected there, and so populations will diverge and differentiate, as they become suited to life in different conditions.

This outline is amplified and explained in the rest of this book. Evolution is a large subject, and difficult to set out as a connected argument. This is because nature is so diverse that exceptions can be found to almost every statement; because evolution involves contributions to and from every branch of biology; and because the argument, like many others in natural science, is circular and can be entered at any point. Here it is entered with the idea of species.

Species

The chicken is the egg's way of ensuring the production of another egg.   Samuel Butler

In 1859, Charles Darwin chose to call his book *The Origin of Species*, and the concept of the biological species is still central to evolutionary thought. Species (the plural is the same) is a Latin word meaning 'kind' or 'sort'. Amongst animals familiar to us, like birds and mammals, the distinction between a blackbird* and a thrush* or a dog and a cat is simple enough. Before Darwin such distinctions were sufficiently explained by the notion that these animals belonged to different species. But what are we recognizing when we learn to call one bird a blackbird and another a thrush? Not simply that these are two kinds of animals which look different, because most people can also recognize male and female blackbirds, and can distinguish a blackbird's nest from a thrush's, by its form and by the eggs it contains. And we also learn that one sort of caterpillar is a cabbage white, while another is a red admiral: surely a blackbird's egg 'is' a blackbird and an acorn 'is' an oak tree, in just the same way.

The relationship that links the acorn and the oak tree, or the caterpillar and the butterfly, gives a clearer picture of the biological species. It is a community of plants or animals in which each member is the offspring of two earlier members, and is in turn capable of producing other members by mating within the community. This idea of species – interbreeding communities extending in successive generations through time – can only apply to organisms with the two-parent pattern of descent with which we are familiar. Where an organism always reproduces asexually, by budding or splitting, or self-fertilizing, for example, the offspring of each parent will be isolated for ever from the rest of the community (Fig. 1). We cannot apply a biological species concept (potential interbreeding community) to such organisms and must rely on physical similarities to recognize species. There are many species reproducing in this way but few are entirely without some sort of sexual process, and those that are may not have much of a future (see section 13.4).

The idea behind the biological species – community of descent

*Blackbird, song thrush and mistle thrush are the English names for three biological species which also live in many other countries, and have names in the language of each. In biology the convention is to give each species a name consisting of two Latin or latinized words: the first, with an initial capital, is the generic name (of a *genus*), and may be shared by several species (see section 11.1, on classification), and the second is the specific name. The blackbird is *Turdus merula*, the song thrush is *Turdus philomelos* and the mistle thrush *Turdus viscivorus*. The advantage of these names is that a Russian or Chinese biologist will understand them as precisely as an Englishman or a Frenchman.

rather than community of resemblance – can be applied to all kinds of organisms, including simple types that cannot readily be separated into species by the sort of observations that enable us to distinguish thrushes and blackbirds. The test, in doubtful cases, is the capacity to interbreed and produce healthy, fertile offspring. Thus, all human races are fully inter-fertile, and so all belong to a single species. A cross between a male donkey and a female horse produces vigorous off-spring, the mule, but all mules are sterile, so that no mixed race can result, and so we know horses and donkeys are different species. On the other hand, the chiffchaff and willow warbler, common English birds, are so similar that it was not until the late eighteenth century, when Gilbert White of Sel-borne noticed a difference in song, that they were suspected to be different. It is now known that they never interbreed in nature, and behave as separate species. The mosquitoes which transmit malaria in Europe provide a more complicated example. Early attempts to control malaria by eliminating the mosquito met with little success. Intensive study showed that much of the anti-mosquito campaign had been wrongly directed. What at first seemed to be a single species of mos-quito, *Anopheles maculipennis*, was resolved into six quite dis-tinct species. The adults of these species are virtually indis-tinguishable, but the eggs and larvae differ, and each species

A   **B**

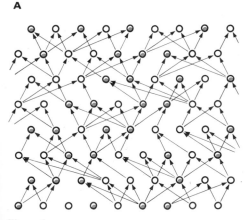

Figure 1

Population structure in sexual and asexual species. A, a sexual species, like our own, in which each individual has two parents of different sexes (white or green blobs). B, an asexual species in which the parent reproduces by dividing into two, as in simple plants and animals like amoeba; each individual has only one parent. According to the theory of evolution, the history of life is a pattern like this, in which the blobs are species, not individuals.

If the population is to remain constant from generation to generation, only half the individuals in B may reproduce. In A, a parent produces more than two offspring only at the expense of others.

has its own geographic range, breeding and feeding behaviour, tolerance of salt water, and so on. The importance of this work to malaria control is that only three of the six species transmit malaria. From our point of view, the important thing is that these six species are real, non-interbreeding units, only recognized after long study: species are real, not a human concept that we try to impose on nature.

I do not pretend that the ability to interbreed is an infallible test, or a definition, of species. No one has yet succeeded in producing a definition of species that covers all cases. But definitions are usually only interesting to those who wish to quarrel with them. And if Darwin is right, that all species are the product of gradual change, we should expect to find examples of species in the making, which can be distinguished only arbitrarily or with difficulty. It remains true that species are real, distinct units in nature.

If the living world can be partitioned into species in this way, then the first question we should ask is not whether such communities change through time (evolution), but why they remain distinct, and how it is that perfect copies of the parents are produced, generation after generation. Such questions, which perplexed Darwin, have been answered by the study of heredity, discussed in chapter 4. But before starting on the intricacies of genetics, there are other questions to be asked about species: are they all of the same sort? And what variations exist between members of one species?

3 Variation within species

We can speak of offspring as perfect copies of their parents. In our own species, we know that this copying is not exact, otherwise we should have trouble recognizing our friends and families. Nevertheless, these imperfections in copying are usually in the finer details – shade of eyes and hair, or cast of features. If we imagine having to recognize our friends by their feet, not their faces, we realize how finely-tuned is our appreciation of human variation: presented with a brood of houseflies, we would be ready to admit the perfection of the copying process, as would a member of another species looking at our own. But because our appreciation of variation is keenest within our own species, it is helpful to use that species as an example of the kinds of variation found in nature. Such natural variation seems to fall into three categories: individual variation, geographic variation, and polymorphism (the co-existence of two or more well-marked varieties in the same district). The most conspicuous variation of all occurs not in nature, but under the artificial conditions of domestication: this is a fourth category.

3·1   Individual variation

In the human species this includes the sort of variation that enables us to recognize acquaintances and public figures – differences in features, stature, voice and so on. More precise indications of the uniqueness of each person come from fingerprints: the prints of only one or two fingers may be sufficient to trace an individual. Recent work on the analysis of blood and body fluids by electrophoresis (separating proteins by differences in their response to an electric field) shows that we also have 'chemical fingerprints', as unique as those on our hands; the fact that skin grafts cannot normally be made from one person to another is due to this chemical individuality.

This kind of analysis has not yet been taken so far in other species as it has in man, but it is already evident that similar

5

variations exist in many animals, so that individuals are unique in several recognizable ways.

3·2   Geographic variation

In general, geographic variation within a species is on a larger scale and involves more obvious differences than the details which distinguish individuals from the same region. In man, the difference between the races – Africans, Caucasians, Orientals and so on – is primarily a geographic phenomenon. This is not so obvious now, after several centuries of increasingly rapid transportation, but the early navigators had no difficulty in observing it. The differences between human races are far more obvious than those between individuals of any one race, but they concern relatively few features – skin coloration, stature, hair form and colour, some facial characteristics, etc. And while the differences between individuals of one race may seem to be random and without function, some of the differences between human races are adaptations to climate or other conditions. For example, an explanation for difference in skin colour between human races is that in the tropics dark skin is advantageous since it shields the underlying tissues from sunburn; but in high latitudes, where sunburn is less of a danger, enough of the ultraviolet component of sunlight must reach the tissues to produce vitamin D (deficiency in vitamin D results in rickets, and the vitamin is synthesized with the help of ultraviolet radiation), so pale, translucent skin is an advantage.

Turning to other species, we find just the same phenomena: individuals of a species from one region may be hard to distinguish, but those from widely separated regions can often be differentiated readily, and may differ in features which are adapted to local conditions. Examples are legion, and are found in every type of animal and plant. Amongst familiar animals, a striking example concerns two British birds, the herring gull (*Larus argentatus*) and the lesser black-backed gull (*Larus fuscus*). In north-western Europe the populations of these two gulls are sharply distinct, in appearance, habits, migratory pattern and so on. Interbreeding is possible, and produces fertile offspring, but is very rare in the wild, so that they behave as distinct biological species. Further east in Europe, the herring gull does not occur, and if the lesser black-backed populations of eastern Europe and Asia are examined, it is found that the further east one travels the less the gulls resemble the British population and the more herring gull characteristics they have. Similarly, to the west of the British Isles, the lesser black-back does not occur, but the herring gull can be traced across the Atlantic and north America, where it becomes more like the lesser black-back. In Siberia there are populations which are roughly intermediate between the two western European species (Fig. 2).

This situation, where two apparently distinct species are joined by a series of geographical and structural intermediates, is called a ring-species. Many such cases are known, but the circumpolar distribution of these gulls is the clearest example. To the naturalist who wishes to place the creatures he studies in neat pigeonholes, such species are a problem. But they are welcome to the evolutionist, because if Darwin is right that species change with time and may split into two, we should expect to find that some present-day species are not sharply distinct – some should be in the process of splitting and will present difficult decisions about whether one or more species should be recognized. In these gulls, the decision has been made to call the two terminal, overlapping populations different species and to place the boundary between these species in northern Russia. The various black-backed populations west of this boundary are named as subspecies* of *Larus fuscus* and the light-backed populations to the east of the boundary are subspecies of *Larus argentatus.* But it will be obvious that such decisions are arbitrary. Difficult or arbitrary decisions like this are common; the British Isles, as a series of outliers of continental Europe, provide many examples of terrestrial animals and plants where a European species is represented in mainland Britain and in other British islands by populations which are separated from their neighbours by water barriers. These populations can often be distinguished by small differences in proportions, size, habits and so on. In small mammals, like voles and fieldmice, and small birds, like wrens, many species and subspecies have been named in the various islands, especially in the Shetlands and Hebrides. The decision whether these are distinct biological species or geographical variants of the mainland form is once again arbitrary, because the test of interbreeding could only be made after capturing and transporting individuals, and this treatment could well influence their behaviour in the tests. These examples are

* Subspecies are given a three-word name; for example the British lesser black-back is *Larus fuscus graellsii,* and the Scandinavian form is *Larus fuscus fuscus*

enough to show that geographic variation is widespread, and that the idea of biological species cannot be applied inflexibly to every situation found in nature.

The examples of geographic variation just discussed are not obviously related to environmental differences. But some types of geographic variation are adaptive, and are so widespread that rules have been formulated to describe them. In warm-blooded animals (birds and mammals), members of a species living in high (cold) latitudes are generally larger and have shorter ears, tails and limbs than their relatives in low latitudes. This rule applies to many species of birds and mammals: the advantage of large size and short extremities in cold climates is that they reduce heat loss (because the ratio of surface area, radiating heat, to volume is less in large animals than in small), while in hot climates long extremities and small size increase heat loss. In plants, variations in size, growth rate, chlorophyll content and other features are found in many species according to the altitude at which the population is growing. Continuous geographic variation of this sort, following latitude or altitude, may appear to be only the direct result of the conditions under which an individual develops, but as we shall see in chapter 5, such variations are usually inherited.

Figure 2
Circumpolar ring-species of gulls. The map shows the distribution of some of the subspecies of herring gulls (*Larus argentatus*) and lesser black-backed gulls (*Larus fuscus*). The striped area is the overlap between the two species, and the arrow marks the division between them. Key: 1, herring gull, *Larus argentatus argentatus*; 2, American herring gull, *L. argentatus smithsonianus*; 3, Vega herring gull, *L. argentatus vegae*; 4, Birula's gull, *L. argentatus birulae*; 5, Heuglin's gull, *L. fuscus heuglini*; 6, Siberian lesser black-backed gull, *L. fuscus antelius*; 7, lesser black-backed gull, *L. fuscus fuscus/graellsii*.

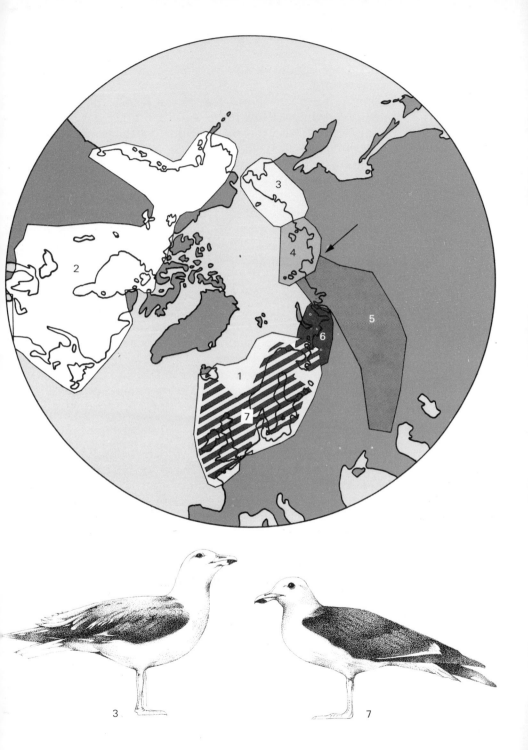

3·3   Polymorphism

This name denotes a situation where two or more clear-cut variants of a species co-exist in the same region. In man, an example is the four blood-groups – A, B, AB and O: every individual belongs to one of these groups, and intermediates do not occur. Hidden polymorphisms like this, only detectable by chemical tests, are frequent in animals and plants, but more attention has been paid to polymorphism in conspicuous features. Such variations can be assumed to be inherited, not determined by the conditions of life, and they are particularly suitable for investigating the effects of natural selection. Examples, discussed in chapter 8, include the snail *Cepaea nemoralis*, common in England, which is polymorphic for the colour of the shell and for the presence or absence of dark bands around the shell (Fig. 28); and the peppered moth, *Biston betularia*, which is polymorphic for wing colour, with pale and dark forms (Fig. 26). In these examples, the different variants have advantages under certain environmental conditions (see chapter 8). The adaptive significance of the human ABO blood-group system is not clear, but the incidence of some diseases (such as ulcers) is greater in O group individuals than in AB, while AB individuals are more susceptible to other diseases (diabetes and smallpox) than are those with blood-group O.

Figure 3
Mimicry in African butterflies.
The butterflies on the right are female *Papilio dardanus*. The top three are mimics, beside the distasteful danaids that they copy. Male *Papilio dardanus* is at bottom left. The three danaid species are (top to bottom) *Danaus chrysippus*, *Amauris echeria* and *A. niavius*.

One particularly intricate type of adaptive polymorphism is found in butterflies such as the African *Papilio dardanus* (Fig. 3). Here, the males are all of one type (monomorphic), but the females occur in several forms, very different from the males and each other. Each of these conspicuous female variants resembles a different species of another group of butterflies, the danaids. These are protected from predators such as birds by being unpleasant to taste. *Papilio dardanus* is not distasteful, but the various female mimics are protected because they will be avoided by birds which have learned not to eat the distasteful danaids. If the mimics were as numerous as the danaid models, birds would be slow to learn to associate the wing pattern with distaste – they would occasionally eat a tasty *Papilio*. But by imitating several different species, the polymorphic female *Papilio dardanus* maintains a larger protected population.

3·4   Variation under domestication

Darwin used variation in domestic animals as one of the major arguments for his theory. The science of genetics was unknown then, and domestic animals and plants were the only source of reliable information about patterns of inheritance. As early as 1840 Darwin produced an elaborate questionnaire on animal breeding for circulation to stockbreeders and others. Darwin bred pigeons himself, and made good use of his knowledge of them in *The Origin of Species*. When John Murray, his publisher, submitted the manuscript of that book to the Rev. Whitwell Elwin, a respected scholar, for an opinion of its worth, Elwin suggested that Darwin confine himself to pigeons, writing 'Everybody is interested in pigeons. The book would be reviewed in every journal in the kingdom, and would soon be on every library table.' The second sentence, at least, was prophetic.

The most striking example of variation in domestic animals is surely the amazing range of dogs. Darwin thought that the various breeds of dog were descended from several different wild species. He gave no good reason for this opinion, and it seems that he was simply unable to believe that a single species could be the source of such variety. Modern opinion is that the domestic dog is descended from the wolf, *Canis lupus*. Archaeological finds prove that dogs have been domesticated for at least 14 000 years. We do not know whether wolves were domesticated once or several times, or where the original domestication took place, although it must have been in the northern hemisphere, the home of the wolf. Dogs have since been distributed all over the world by man, and in many places they have escaped and assumed the status of a wild species, like the dingo in Australia.

So men have been breeding and selecting dogs for at least 14 000 years. The results of this selection are too familiar to need description. All breeds of dog are interfertile, but some crosses, for example between a one-kilogram chihuahua and a great dane weighing seventy-five times as much, are prevented by the great disparity in size. A cross between a great dane and a St Bernard results in seriously defective offspring, but this is not because the parents belong to different species; it is because each of these breeds has been selected for giant size as far as it will go, and crossing these two specialized lines of giants results in partial breakdown of the mechanism of development. In the same way, bulldogs have been selected for their peculiar characteristics to the point where many males are infertile.

We can take the breeds of dog as an indication of the potential variability inherent in a single species of mammal. This variation is genetic, since it breeds true. In dogs, the range of form is very great because selection has been guided not only by the desire to fit form to function, as in working dogs, but also, in 'toy' breeds, by whim or fashion. In other domesticated mammals, such as horses, pigs and sheep, the variation produced by selective breeding from single wild species is striking (compare a racehorse with a Shetland pony), but not so great as in dogs. This may be because these animals have been bred for use, not caprice, and perhaps because they have not been domesticated for so long as the dog (the earliest remains of domestic pigs and cattle are about 8500 years old).

Darwin's account of pigeon breeds (often selected, like dogs, for fancy rather than use) shows that bird species have as much potential variability as mammals. The work of agriculturists with cereals and other vegetables, and of geneticists with insects, seems to confirm that great potential variability is a feature of all species.

Figure 4
A wolf, *Canis lupus*, and an assortment of domestic dogs, all descended from the wild species.

This survey of species and their variation can be summed up as a series of statements, which in turn provoke questions to be answered by the study of heredity.

1. Definition of the biological species as an interbreeding community does not always work perfectly. In some cases, decisions about the limits of species are arbitrary.
What mechanisms cause members of a species to develop as near-perfect copies of their parents?
What prevents members of different species from interbreeding?
Are there genetic mechanisms that allow some individuals to interbreed successfully, and prevent others from doing so?

2. Within a species, each individual is usually unique, characterized by variations in structure and chemistry.
Are these variations inherited? And if so, what is their source?

3. Many species contain recognizable geographic races or subspecies, often adapted to local conditions.
Are these adaptations inherited, or induced by those conditions?

4. Many species are polymorphic, with clear-cut variants living together in the same region.
How are these variations inherited and maintained?

5. Domestication shows that wild species contain enormous potential heritable variation.
What is the source of this variation, and why is it not manifested in the wild?

4 Heredity

The laws governing inheritance are quite unknown.

Charles Darwin, *The Origin of Species*
A great man of science ... knows everything about everything, except why a hen's egg don't turn into a crocodile, and two or three other little things. Charles Kingsley, *The Water Babies*

We recognize biological species as communities of descent. In most species which breed sexually, the only material that passes from the parents to the next generation is the minute quantity contained in the egg and sperm (in man, for example, the egg cell is about 0·1 mm across and the sperm is very much smaller). The vast majority of species do not care for their young as do birds and mammals – the fertilized egg is left to take care of itself. Since such eggs develop into copies of the parents, they must contain instructions for producing that pattern.

Darwin was completely ignorant of the way in which these instructions are passed from generation to generation, despite his experience in breeding animals and plants. He knew that inheritance is often 'blending' – the offspring being 'of mixed blood', intermediate between the parents – but he also knew of many exceptions to that rule. He believed that characters acquired during the life of an organism, such as parts or organs enlarged by use, or weakened by disuse, were transmitted to the offspring, and in 1868 published a theory to account for this. He proposed that all parts of an organism secrete minute granules throughout life, and that these granules circulate around the body and accumulate in the reproductive organs, ready to be passed on to the next generation. But two years before this, in 1866, Gregor Mendel (Fig. 70) published an account of a long series of breeding experiments with pea plants from which he developed a theory that explained many of Darwin's difficulties. Unfortunately, the significance of Mendel's work was not noticed by Darwin, or any other scientist, until 1900, when both Mendel and Darwin were dead.

4·1 Mendel's theory

To proceed further with the problem 'What is a species?' as distinct from the other problem 'How do species survive?' we must go back and take up the thread of the enquiry exactly where Mendel dropped it. William Bateson, 1901

Mendel experimented with varieties of garden peas (*Pisum sativum*) from seedsmen. He found varieties showing clear-cut differences in such features as flower colour (white versus purple), seed colour (green v. yellow) and form of seed (round v. wrinkled), and grew each for two years to make sure that each variety was pure, that is, it bred true. He chose pea plants because the flower is normally self-fertilized, but can be cross-fertilized experimentally if the stamens are removed before they ripen.

In a typical experiment (Fig. 5) he cross-fertilized the flowers of plants grown from green and yellow seeds, examined the resulting hybrid seeds (peas) and found that they were all yellow*. He then planted these peas, allowed the plants to self-fertilize, and again examined the seeds produced. He found that these hybrid plants, grown from yellow seed, did not breed true. Out of 8023 peas in this second generation, 6022 were yellow and 2001 green. He noticed that these figures are a very close approximation to a ratio of three yellow to one green. Again, he planted these peas and allowed the second generation plants to self-fertilize. He found that the green peas always bred true, but that the yellow ones did not. Out of 519 second generation yellow peas, 166 bred true but 353 did not: the latter group again produced yellow and green seeds in the proportion of three to one. When a plant yielded yellow and green seeds, the different types were found randomly distributed in the pod: a pod might contain five or six yellow and two or three green peas.

Mendel's fame is due to the theory he thought out to explain these facts. First, since a cross between the pure-bred yellow line and the pure-bred green produced all yellow peas, he supposed that the character 'yellow' was *dominant* (symbolized by 'A' in Figure 5) over 'green', which he called *recessive* (symbolized by 'a'). Since a hybrid yellow pea can produce both green and yellow offspring, it must carry the 'green' character in latent form. To explain this, he proposed that each pea and plant carries a double dose of characters or hereditary factors (now called *genes*), so that pure-bred yellow could be symbolized by AA, pure-bred green by aa. The pollen and egg-cells would carry only one factor, A or a. The first generation peas

15

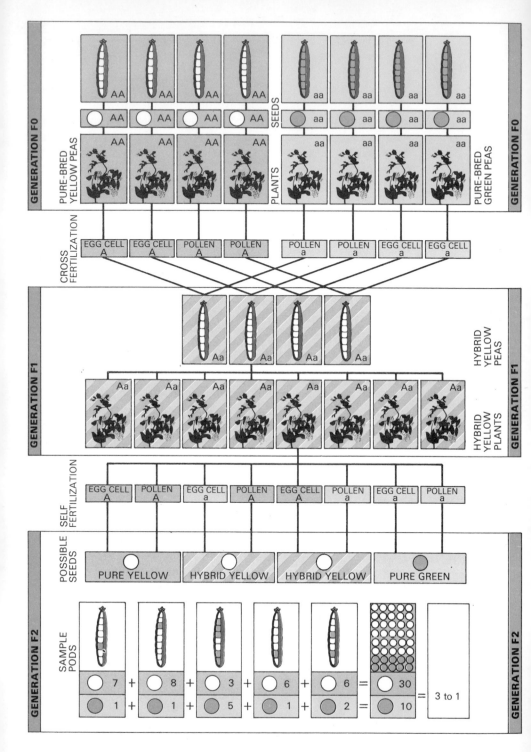

in his experiment (F_1 in Fig. 5), all yellow, would then be Aa, having received 'A' (in pollen or egg-cell) from one parent and 'a' from the other. The second generation, produced by self-fertilization of the first, would then have an equal chance of receiving either 'A' or 'a' in both the pollen and the egg-cell, and so should be $\frac{1}{4}$AA (pure-breeding yellow), $\frac{1}{2}$Aa (like their parents, impure breeding yellow) and $\frac{1}{4}$aa (pure-breeding green): thus the second generation should contain $\frac{3}{4}$ yellow ($\frac{1}{4}$AA + $\frac{1}{2}$Aa) and $\frac{1}{4}$ green (aa), and the 3:1 ratio that Mendel observed would be explained. By a series of crosses between plants of each constitution Mendel was able to test this theory, and to show that it accounted for all the available facts. He also found that reciprocal crosses (pollen from green crossed with egg-cell from yellow; yellow pollen with green egg-cell) proved that the allocation of the genetic factors (A or a) to the pollen and egg-cells (male and female sex cells or *gametes*) is random, so that each gamete has an equal chance of receiving either factor. Fertilization is also random, an egg-cell with A having an equal chance of being fertilized by pollen with A or a.

Mendel's experiments merit description, because most subsequent work in genetics has been based on his principles and practices. The great advances that he made were his ideas of dominant and recessive factors (*genes*); the double dose of factors in an organism, so that an organism can be hybrid; the random segregation of single factors to the gametes, so that a gamete is always pure, carrying one factor or the other; and the transmission of the factors, unchanged and uncontaminated, from generation to generation. Mendel showed that inheritance is not blending, as Darwin supposed, but particulate (of course, Mendel's particles, the genes, are nothing to do with the mythical 'granules' that Darwin supposed were given off by all parts of the organism). One other point of great importance that follows from Mendel's theory is the clear distinction between the physical appearance of an organism (called its *phenotype*) and its genetic constitution (the *genotype*), because yellow peas (phenotype) may have the genotype AA or Aa. More plainly, the caterpillar, the chrysalis and the butterfly are three different phenotypes, all expressing the same genotype.

Mendel also conducted more complicated experiments involving two pairs of factors, for example crossing pea plants grown

Figure 5
Mendel's experiments with green and yellow peas.
F_0, F_1 and F_2 are the symbols used in genetics for the parental, first and second generations. The proportion of three yellow to one green in the F_2 generation is an ideal result, and would only be approximated in actual experiments.

17

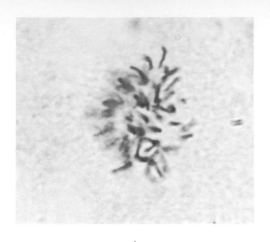
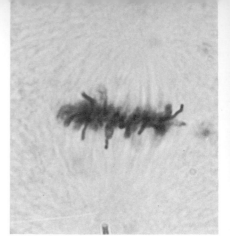

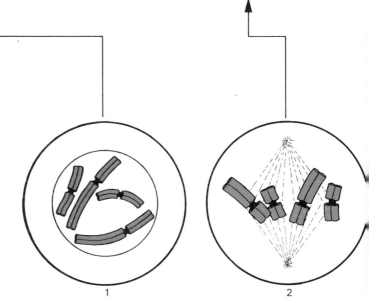

Figure 6
Mitosis, the process
of cell division.
The numbered
diagrams, explained
in the text (p. 21), show
stages of mitosis in a
cell with four
chromosomes. Above
them are
corresponding stages
in embryo trout
(*Salmo trutta*)
enlarged about 2000
times. Trout cells
have about eighty
chromosomes. The
photographs are from
stained slices through
the cells, and not all
the chromosomes are
visible.

1

2

from pure-bred yellow, wrinkled seeds with plants grown from
green, smooth seeds. He found that the yellow/green pair of
factors and the wrinkled/smooth pair were inherited independently.

Subsequent experiments have confirmed all these aspects of
Mendel's work, and shown that his principles can be applied
in all sexual organisms. However, it is found that clear-cut
dominant/recessive systems involving a single pair of factors
are not all that common. In many attributes, such as height
in human beings, the offspring are roughly intermediate
between the parents. But analysis shows that this apparent

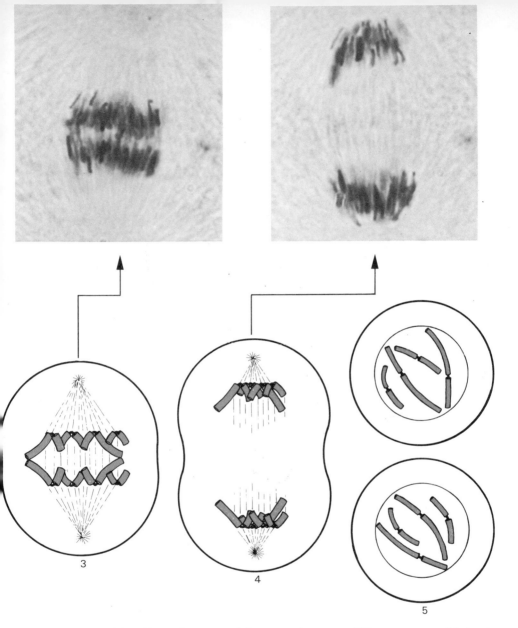

blending of parental features is not a different type of inheritance: it involves attributes which are controlled by several or many Mendelian genes, with additive effects. The rule that different pairs of factors are inherited independently has also been found to have many exceptions: factors tend to be transmitted in groups, called *linkage groups*. These, and other apparent anomalies, were explained by microscopic study of the cells of organisms.

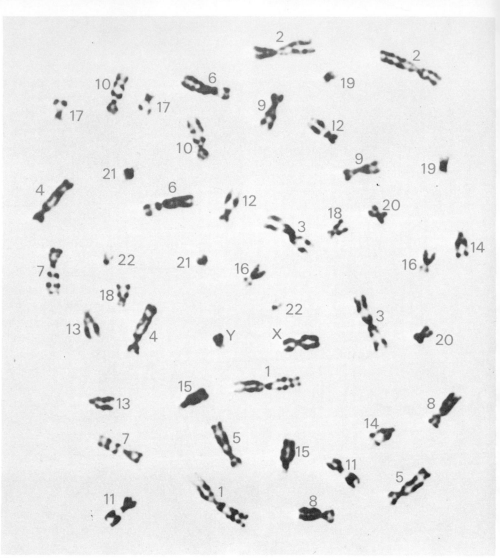

Figure 7

The chromosomes of a human cell enlarged about 3300 times. In this preparation a cell undergoing mitosis has been squashed to spread out the chromosomes, and stained. There are 22 numbered pairs of chromosomes, matching in size and shape, and two chromosomes (X, Y) which do not match – 46 in all. The X and Y chromosomes are those responsible for sex determination. In all mammals, XY individuals are male, and XX are female. All egg-cells contain a single X chromosome, and males produce sperm which are 50 per cent X-bearing and 50 per cent Y-bearing. As a result, fertilized eggs are 50 per cent XX and 50 per cent XY, and the sex ratio is maintained.

Other groups of animals, such as birds and butterflies, have a different system in which males have a matching pair of sex chromosomes, and females have unlike sex chromosomes (butterflies) or only one sex chromosome (birds); in either case a 50:50 sex ratio results.

4·2 The chromosome theory

By 1900, when Mendel's work was rediscovered, a quite different line of investigation could be brought into genetic theory: direct observation of cells under the microscope.

All organisms are composed of one or more cells, and all plant and animal cells consist of two zones, an outer zone, the *cytoplasm*, containing the various organelles (microscopic organs) concerned with the life processes of the cell, and an inner zone, the *nucleus*, which is concerned with reproduction.

The first insight into the role of the nucleus came from study of its behaviour when the cell divides. Cell division is going on all the time in our bodies: growth, repair and replacement of tissues are all accomplished by increase in number of cells. In a resting (non-dividing) cell, the nucleus is a dense or dark globule with granular contents. When a cell enters the active, dividing phase, the contents of the nucleus become organized into a number of threads, the *chromosomes* ('coloured bodies', so named because of their affinity for the dyes used to make cell contents visible under the microscope). Each chromosome can be seen to consist of two separate threads (*chromatids*), held together at one point (Fig. 6·1). Next, the chromosomes contract and thicken by coiling, the envelope bounding the nucleus disappears, and a spindle-shaped structure, formed of minute tubules, develops. The chromosomes then attach to the central plane or equator of the spindle (Fig. 6·2), the two chromatids composing each chromosome separate (Fig. 6·3) and are drawn towards the poles of the spindle (Fig. 6·4) as two sets of new, daughter chromosomes. The spindle disappears, a new nuclear envelope appears around each of the new sets of chromosomes, and the whole cell now divides into two (Fig. 6·5). Finally, the chromosomes become less easily visible, and replicate, each one producing two chromatids, during the resting stage.

This extraordinary sequence of events, called *mitosis*, happens every time a plant or animal cell divides. It was soon realized that the number of chromosomes in dividing nuclei is constant for each species, and that these numbers are even. Man, for example, has 46 chromosomes in each cell (Fig. 7), while the small fruit-fly *Drosophila*, the favourite experimental animal of geneticists, has six to twelve, depending on the species

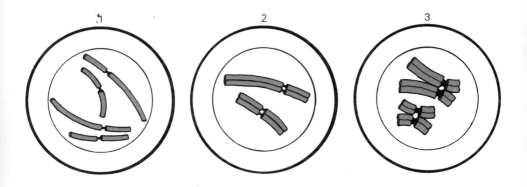

Figure 8
Meiosis, the special cycle of cell division that
produces gametes (egg and sperm cells).
The numbered diagrams, explained in the text,
show stages of meiosis in a cell with four
chromosomes. Further details of meiosis are shown
in Figure 15.

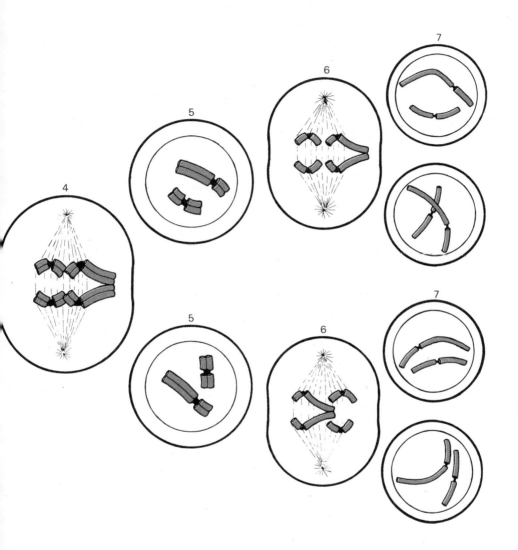

(Fig. 17). It can also be seen that the chromosomes fall into pairs, the members of each pair matched in size and shape. These regularities in number and behaviour of chromosomes suggested that they might be the carriers of the hereditary material. The matter was clinched by observations of chromosomes in the development of gametes (sperm and egg-cells).

In the reproductive organs (testis and ovary in animals, spore-producing organs in plants), those cells which are to produce gametes go through a cycle of division, called *meiosis* ('lessening'), which differs from the mitotic cycle, just described, of non-reproductive cells. When a sperm or egg mother-cell enters the active phase of division, chromosomes become visible in the nucleus, as in mitosis, but each chromosome appears single, and is not split into two separate threads (Fig. 8·1). Instead, the chromosomes associate in like-sized pairs (Fig. 8·2), of the sort numbered in Figure 7. Each chromosome now splits into two chromatids (Fig.8·3), as in early mitosis, so that each chromosome-pair contains four threads, more or less tangled together. A spindle appears, the chromosome-pairs attach to its equator and then separate, one of each pair being drawn towards each pole of the spindle (Fig. 8·4).

The essential feature of meiosis is that in this division it is paired chromosomes that move apart, each containing two threads, whereas in mitosis it is the two threads of each chromosome that separate. After the first division of meiosis two new nuclei are formed (Fig. 8·5), each containing half the number of chromosomes present in the parent nucleus – four in *Drosophila melanogaster*, 23 in man – and these chromosomes are already divided into two chromatids. The two new nuclei immediately undergo a second division, resembling mitosis in that individual chromosomes attach to the spindle, and the two chromatids of each are drawn apart (Fig. 8·6). The end result of this meiotic cycle is four nuclei, each with half the number of chromosomes of the parent cell (Fig. 8·7). In male organisms, each of these four nuclei develops into a sperm. In most female organisms three of the nuclei degenerate and one becomes the unfertilized egg.

When fertilization occurs, the egg-cell is penetrated by a sperm and the nucleus of the sperm fuses with that of the egg. Because each of these two nuclei had half the number of chromosomes typical for the species, the resulting fertilized egg or *zygote* has the full complement, half of them from each parent. This full complement of chromosomes is called the *diploid* number, and the half-complement found in gametes is the *haploid* number.

These complex nuclear manoeuvres are a perfect explanation of Mendel's theory, which was proposed before anything was known about chromosomes. Mendel guessed that each individual has a double dose of factors, that the factors segregate independently and at random in the gametes, and that they recombine in the next generation: this is an exact description of the behaviour of chromosomes. To be more explicit, the fact that organisms have an even number of chromosomes in each nucleus, and that these chromosomes fall into matched pairs (called *homologous* pairs) is due to the organism receiving one of each matched pair from the mother and one from the father. The separation of these pairs in the first division of meiosis, one to each daughter nucleus, results in a random combination of maternal and paternal chromosomes, so that the four chromosomes in the egg-cell of *Drosophila melanogaster*, for example, may be one paternal and three maternal, or two of each, or any other combination (exceptions to this rule are discussed in section 5·4). The linkage between the inheritance of some genetic factors, mentioned at the end of the previous section, is also explained: linked genes are to be found on the same chromosome.

The theory that the chromosomes carry the hereditary material was the basis of genetics for the first half of this century, and was greatly refined by breeding experiments and observations of nuclear division. These refinements resulted in the concept of the chromosome as a thread with the genes arranged like beads along it. In the fly *Drosophila* the system of inheritance became so well understood, after many thousands of experiments, that 'maps' of each chromosome could be drawn, with the relative position of the genes for various characters marked in. But there was still a great gap in genetic theory: what were these genes, and how did a gene control or direct the features of organisms? These questions were finally answered not by breeding experiments or observations under the microscope, but by work at the molecular level, in chemistry rather than biology.

4·3   DNA and the genetic code

Soon after the chromosome theory of heredity became established, early in this century, the gross chemical composition of chromosomes was worked out. They were found to have two main components, *nucleic acid* and *protein*. Since nucleic acids were known to be relatively uniform compounds, while proteins are extremely varied, it was naturally thought that the hereditary material was the protein part of the chromosome. Although this idea turned out to be wrong, it is worth making a short digression on proteins.

Proteins are chemical compounds which are produced only by living organisms. They are large, chain-like molecules built up of small sub-units called *amino acids*, of which there are twenty different sorts. Natural protein molecules may contain any combination of these units, linked end to end. The resulting protein chain, which may be of any length, is folded into a complicated three-dimensional pattern which is specific for each protein (Fig. 9). Because each link in the protein chain may be any one of the twenty different amino acids, the variety of possible proteins is inconceivably large. A protein molecule 100 links long, a typical size for a natural protein, could have 20^{100} possible configurations, a number far larger than the total number of atoms in the universe.

Proteins are the major component of living tissue. They include structural materials (e.g. keratin, which forms the hair of mammals and the feathers of birds, and collagen, which forms the framework of our bones and teeth) and transporters (e.g. haemoglobin, the red protein which carries oxygen in our blood). But the most important class of proteins is the *enzymes* – proteins which act as very efficient catalysts, facilitating chemical reactions which would otherwise take place very slowly or not at all. Enzymes occur in organisms in enormous variety, each one specific for a certain reaction. Most of the life processes of organisms consist of chemical pathways, where each step in the path is a reaction mediated by a different enzyme. Some idea of the importance and variety of proteins comes from the estimate that each cell in our bodies contains at least 10 000 different types of protein.

Because of this enormous variety, proteins were obviously candidates for carrying genetic messages. But by the early

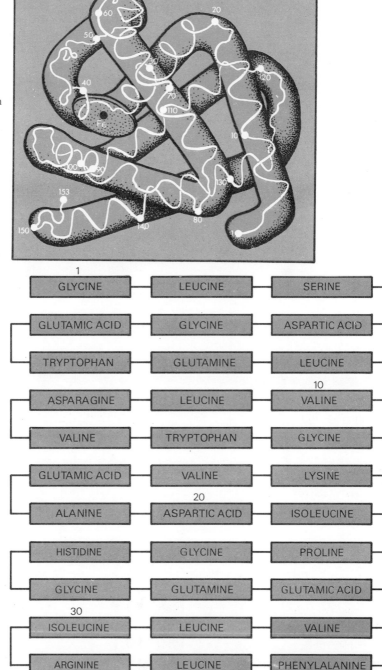

Figure 9

The molecule of the protein myoglobin. The structure is shown at three different levels. The folded sausage (green) gives an idea of the form of the molecule and of the position of the oxygen-carrying haem group (the coin-like shape), containing an iron atom (Fe). The white coiled line within the sausage is a more accurate representation of the chain of amino acids. The chain contains 153 amino acids (the first, last and every tenth one are numbered), and is partly spiral, partly angular or irregular. Below, the first 33 amino acids of human myoglobin.

1		
GLYCINE	LEUCINE	SERINE
GLUTAMIC ACID	GLYCINE	ASPARTIC ACID
TRYPTOPHAN	GLUTAMINE	LEUCINE
ASPARAGINE	LEUCINE	VALINE
VALINE	TRYPTOPHAN	GLYCINE
GLUTAMIC ACID	VALINE	LYSINE
ALANINE	ASPARTIC ACID	ISOLEUCINE
HISTIDINE	GLYCINE	PROLINE
GLYCINE	GLUTAMINE	GLUTAMIC ACID
ISOLEUCINE	LEUCINE	VALINE
ARGININE	LEUCINE	PHENYLALANINE

10 (above VALINE, row 4)
20 (above ASPARTIC ACID, row 7)
30 (above ISOLEUCINE, row 10)

27

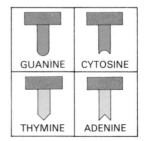

Figure 10
The structure of the
DNA molecule.
The diagrams are
simplified versions of
the Watson-Crick
model, showing the
sugar/phosphate side-
pieces as spiral tubes,
and the two types of
base-pair cross-pieces
as interlocking
planks. The lower
diagram shows
reproduction or
replication of the
molecule. Alongside
each strand of the old
molecule a new
strand is forming
from sugar,
phosphate and base
molecules, shown as
building blocks, ready
for incorporation.
The proportions of
the diagram (the
width of the spiral,
ten base-pairs to each
complete turn) are
correct, but the way
they are represented
does not correspond
to anything visible or
'real'.

GUANINE | CYTOSINE

THYMINE | ADENINE

28

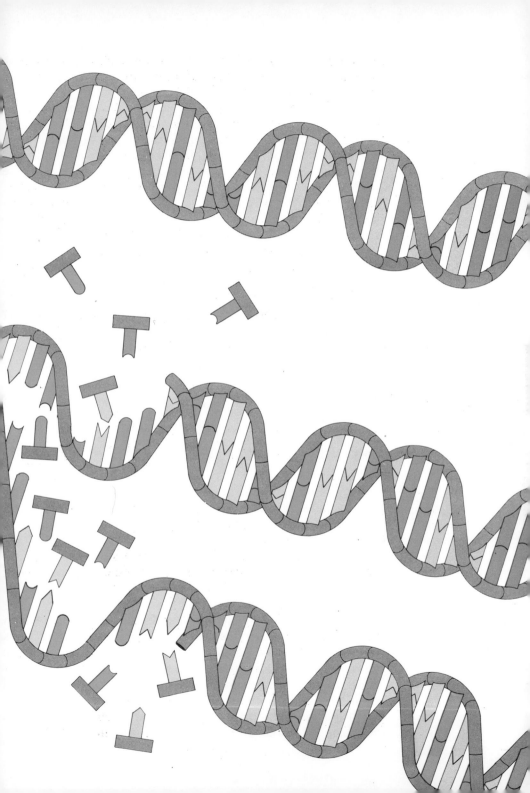

1950s experimental evidence had accumulated to show that the other component of chromosomes, nucleic acid, must be the hereditary material. Nucleic acids are of two types, *ribonucleic acid* (RNA for short) and *deoxyribonucleic acid* (DNA). RNA is found outside the nucleus, and DNA within the nucleus, in the chromosomes. Both types of nucleic acid are long molecules, with a chain-like backbone consisting of alternate phosphate and sugar sub-units. (The sugar is ribose in RNA, deoxyribose in DNA, hence the names of the nucleic acids.) Attached to each sugar sub-unit there is a base, the chemical term for a class of molecules including alkalis. In DNA there are four different bases – adenine, cytosine, guanine and thymine. Although the chemical composition of DNA was well known, there was no indication of how the substance could have a genetic function. But in 1953, Francis Crick and James Watson (Fig. 71) proposed a model for the structure of the DNA molecule which showed how it could contain long, coded messages. This model – the double helix – with its biological implications ranks as the greatest contribution to biology since the work of Darwin and Mendel.

The Watson–Crick model of the DNA molecule (Fig. 10) can be thought of as a free-standing spiral staircase, in which the two strings or side-pieces are long chains of alternate sugars and phosphates, and each tread is formed by two bases, linking the side chains. These treads are of just two types, because the four bases pair only in two ways – adenine always bonded to thymine, and guanine to cytosine – but these base-pairs may occur in any sequence, and may be orientated either way round (for example, in the adenine–thymine bond the adenine may be on the left or right side of the tread). This model has two most significant features. First, it offers a simple mechanism for replication (reproduction) of the molecule – by progressive separation of the bonds between the bases, so that the double helix 'unzips' and uncoils, allowing a new chain to be synthesized in sequence alongside each of the old side chains, which act as moulds or templates (Fig. 10). Second, the model offers a method of carrying coded messages – the sequence of the bases. Along one side chain, there may be any one of the four bases attached to each sugar, and the sequence of the bases could be a coded message written in a four-letter alphabet, which we can symbolize by the initial letters of the bases (adenine – A, cytosine – C, guanine – G, thymine – T).

These implications of the model stimulated intense investigation, and within about a dozen years this code (the *genetic code*) had been cracked, and the way in which it is read and translated had been worked out. With a four-letter alphabet, there are several ways of writing messages: if the letters are read individually, only four different statements will be possible; if they are read in pairs there are sixteen possible statements (AC, AG, AT, AA, CT, CG, CC, CA, etc.); if read in threes, 64, and so on. The genetic code turns out to be the same in all organisms, so far as we know, and to be in non-overlapping triplets. For example, the base sequence TAG CATACT would be read as the three words 'tag', 'cat' and 'act'. In such a code there are 64 possible statements. With this limited language, it is obvious that those statements must be very simple. In fact there are only two types of statement: one specifies an amino acid, and one is a stop sign. There are twenty different amino acids and a stop sign is unambiguous, so that the whole genetic language only needs 21 different statements. Many of the 64 possible messages in the triplet code are therefore redundant, and it turns out that several have the same meaning. There are three different triplets meaning stop, and the remaining 61 are distributed amongst the amino acids, some acids being coded by as many as six different triplets (Fig. 11).

The simplicity of this arrangement is surely the most stunning knowledge ever to have come out of biology. The only instructions in the genetic code are for assembling proteins. And the extraordinary variety of life seems ultimately to be due solely to differences in amino acid sequences. Genes for 'blue eyes' or 'wrinkled seed coat' do not exist: such features are the phenotypic consequences of a genotype that specifies nothing but proteins.

The way in which the DNA of a cell is read and translated is complicated, and need only be described in outline. In the DNA molecule, it is clear that each genetic message must be contained in one strand of the double helix, because the other strand carries a complementary sequence of bases (T opposite A and G opposite C, and vice versa), which will code quite a different message, presumably nonsensical. But when the molecule reproduces itself, by the 'unzipping' procedure outlined above, a new meaningful message can be laid down on the mould or template formed by this nonsense strand. In the

		SECOND LETTER							
		A		**G**		**T**		**C**	

FIRST LETTER		SECOND LETTER A		SECOND LETTER G		SECOND LETTER T		SECOND LETTER C		THIRD LETTER
A	AAA	Phenylalanine	AGA	Serine	ATA	Tyrosine	ACA	Cysteine	A
	AAG	Phenylalanine	AGG	Serine	ATG	Tyrosine	ACG	Cysteine	G
	AAT	Leucine	AGT	Serine	ATT	Stop	ACT	Stop	T
	AAC	Leucine	AGC	Serine	ATC	Stop	ACC	Tryptophan	C
G	GAA	Leucine	GGA	Proline	GTA	Histidine	GCA	Arginine	A
	GAG	Leucine	GGG	Proline	GTG	Histidine	GCG	Arginine	G
	GAT	Leucine	GGT	Proline	GTT	Glutamine	GCT	Arginine	T
	GAC	Leucine	GGC	Proline	GTC	Glutamine	GCC	Arginine	C
T	TAA	Isoleucine	TGA	Threonine	TTA	Asparagine	TCA	Serine	A
	TAG	Isoleucine	TGG	Threonine	TTG	Asparagine	TCG	Serine	G
	TAT	Isoleucine	TGT	Threonine	TTT	Lysine	TCT	Arginine	T
	TAC	Methionine	TGC	Threonine	TTC	Lysine	TCC	Arginine	C
C	CAA	Valine	CGA	Alanine	CTA	Aspartic Acid	CCA	Glycine	A
	CAG	Valine	CGG	Alanine	CTG	Aspartic Acid	CCG	Glycine	G
	CAT	Valine	CGT	Alanine	CTT	Glutamic Acid	CCT	Glycine	T
	CAC	Valine	CGC	Alanine	CTC	Glutamic Acid	CCC	Glycine	C

Figure 11

The genetic code.
The letters A, G, T and C stand for adenine, guanine, thymine and cytosine, the four bases in DNA. The 64 possible triplet combinations of these letters are shown, together with their meaning – the named amino acid, or 'stop'. Most of the redundancy of the code is in the third letters of the triplets: AG-, GA-, GG-, GC-, TG-, CA-, CG-, and CC- each has the same meaning, regardless of the third letter.

Figure 12

DNA makes RNA.
An electron micrograph of DNA producing ribosomal RNA. The section of DNA 'fibre' shown here contains three genes for ribosomal RNA, out of each of which are growing 80–100 strands of RNA. These strands increase in length from one end of the gene to the other, the longest ones being fully transcribed, and the shortest just beginning transcription. The actual DNA and RNA molecules are not seen here, but the shape of these molecules is made visible by the proteins (enzymes and insulators) attached to them. The preparation is from the ovary of the clawed toad, *Xenopus*, enlarged about 28 500 times. Photograph courtesy of Dr Ulrich Scheer, German Cancer Research Centre, Heidelberg.

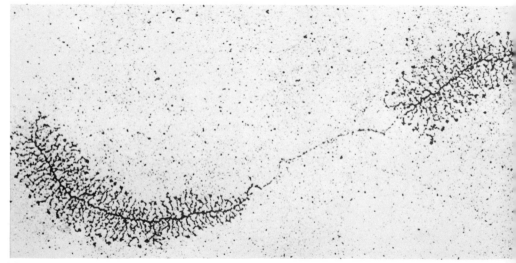

double helix, therefore, one strand carries the message, the other is necessary for replication of the molecule and the message.

Translation of the message is not direct – the amino acids are not assembled into proteins alongside the DNA. Instead, there is a two-phase sequence, *transcription* (reading the message, in the nucleus), and *translation* (acting on the message by synthesizing protein, in the cytoplasm). Both these processes involve the other variety of nucleic acid, ribonucleic acid (RNA). RNA differs from DNA principally in having a single-stranded molecule. It occurs in three varieties – messenger RNA, ribosomal RNA and transfer RNA. In the first phase of reading the message, transcription, an enzyme system attaches to the DNA in the chromosome, and recognizes a section between a start signal (which is not a triplet) and a stop signal. Such a section usually corresponds to one protein. The enzyme system transcribes this section of DNA, base by base, into a newly synthesized molecule of messenger RNA (Fig. 12). The molecule of messenger RNA, containing instructions for one protein, passes out of the nucleus into the cytoplasm and associates with a *ribosome*.

Ribosomes are minute particles which can be visualized as sacs built of proteins and RNA, here in the ribosomal form, and are the site of translation of the message (Fig. 13). The thread-like messenger RNA molecule passes through the ribosome

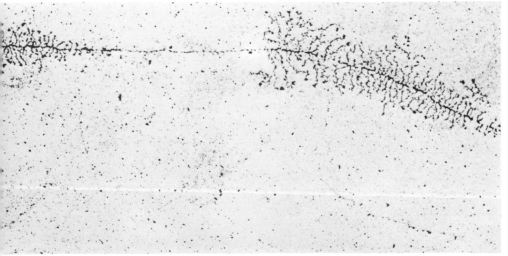

rather like recording tape through the head of a tape recorder, and as it passes through the triplet code is recognized by the third type of RNA, transfer RNA. Transfer RNAs constitute a family of molecules, each adapted to recognize a particular triplet of the code, and to add the appropriate amino acid to the protein chain, which emerges from the ribosome as it is synthesized, link by link.

This is a much-simplified account of a complicated process, involving many different regulating proteins. It is estimated that synthesis of a single protein molecule by this system requires the presence of several hundred different proteins, acting as enzymes in transcription, messenger RNA and amino acid synthesis, ribosomal and transfer RNA activity, and so on. When one realizes that in every cell these proteins themselves must previously have been synthesized by the system, on the basis of information in the DNA, and that the transfer and ribosomal RNA must also be synthesized following information from the nucleus, the mind begins to reel.

From this remarkable new knowledge of heredity at the molecular level, we get a picture of the chromosomes as giant molecules of DNA, each containing a series of recipes for proteins separated by stop and start signs. This picture is certainly oversimplified, because it is known that in many organisms there are long sequences of repetitive DNA, with the same message repeated hundreds, thousands or millions of times, and there are also regions of DNA which are untranscribable, containing only nonsense. Further, we know that each cell in the body of an organism contains a full set of chromosomes, and therefore a full set of instructions for constructing the whole organism. Yet cells become specialized and differentiated; in animals some form muscle cells, others kidney cells, others nerve cells, and so on. So it is evident that these cells are only acting on quite a small part of the genetic message in their nuclei, and that the rest of it is not being read. There are various known mechanisms which prevent transcription of DNA: by analogy with electricity they can be thought of as switches and insulators, and most of them involve binding of protein with the DNA, ensuring that superfluous genes remain inactive. Production of these insulating or repressor proteins is itself the work of genes, and there is probably a hierarchy of control genes of this type, some switching on and off a single gene, and some 'master genes', controlling batteries of genes.

Figure 13

Translation of the genetic code – a diagram of how proteins are produced.

The band across the foot of the diagram represents part of a molecule of messenger RNA, with the four different bases of the code indicated by spikes of different height. The pale grey shapes are ribosomes, and the dark grey rectangles are molecules of transfer RNA, each bearing three spikes which will fit only with a particular triplet in messenger RNA. The green shapes are amino acid molecules. Transfer RNA molecules, each charged with the appropriate amino acid, recognize their triplets on the messenger RNA in the ribosome, and add their amino acids to the growing protein chain. In nature, ribosomes are about 75 'spikes' apart on the messenger RNA molecule, not so close together as in the diagram.

The entire genetic message has so far been worked out only for one type of organism, a virus that infects the human intestinal bacillus, *Escherichia coli*. Viruses hardly merit the name 'organism', for they are only capable of life within the cells of their host, where they make use of the host's genetic machinery. Because of this parasitism at the molecular level, they can do without an elaborate protein-producing apparatus. The virus whose entire DNA has been decoded contains only nine genes, occupying 5375 code-letters (bases). Two stretches of its DNA each contain two overlapping genes: two different messages are encoded in the same series of letters, using different reading-frames. For example, the sequence CATTAGACTG can be read as 'CAT', 'TAG', 'ACT', 'G ...' if reading begins at the first letter, or as 'ATT', 'AGA', 'CTG' if reading begins at the second letter. This overlapping of genes could be a way of economizing on DNA in minute organisms like viruses. Whether gene overlap occurs in higher organisms is not yet known, but they have an additional complication. Recent work on the haemoglobin genes of mice and rabbits, and on the gene for egg-white protein in chickens, shows that the protein-specifying part of the DNA is split into two or more sections, separated by quite long, untranslated regions.

In man, it is estimated that the DNA in each cell is sufficient to code at least five million proteins, allowing about 600 base-pairs (200 triplets) per gene. Yet geneticists guess that 100 000 genes might be about enough to specify a human being. What the rest of the DNA is doing remains unknown. Nor is it yet known precisely how the DNA is packed or arranged in the chromosomes.

To summarize this chapter, we can note some of the ways in which modern molecular genetics has modified previous ideas about heredity. Firstly, we can contrast the Mendelian view of genes as entities which control single characters, like eye colour or flower colour, with the modern idea of genes as segments of DNA molecules, specifying proteins whose interactions may influence eye or flower colour amongst other things. Secondly, the designation of genes as dominant or recessive by Mendel and early geneticists must be modified. These categories referred to visible characters, but those are not the direct product of the genes. In Mendel's experiments with peas, 'yellow' and 'green' must be due to differences in proteins, the 'AA' genotype producing one form, and the 'aa' another. In the 'Aa' genotype, with yellow peas, the 'a' gene produces no visible effects, but at the molecular level the gene is presumably active. 'Recessive' is therefore a relative term: a recessive gene produces no visible effect, but may produce protein. Thirdly, the biological species concept – of interbreeding communities – can be supplemented (but not replaced) by a genetic species concept, of species as *gene-pools* in which the genes reproduce asexually (when DNA replicates) and generate phenotypes (organisms) which can reproduce sexually, so producing new mixtures of genes. Fourthly, the mechanism of transcription and translation of the genetic code seems to be a one-way process: information passes from the DNA into the cell, but there is no known way in which the DNA can be modified by information from the cell. This has an important consequence, for it means that characters acquired during the life of an organism, such as the effects of use or disuse, cannot affect the DNA, and therefore cannot be inherited.

5 Genetics and variation

Any variation which is not inherited is unimportant for us.
Charles Darwin, *The Origin of Species*

With some understanding of the mechanism of heredity, we can now look at the variations found within species in a new light, and answer some of the questions listed at the end of chapter 3 (p. 13). Answering those questions will bring out other aspects of genetics.

Firstly, why do organisms develop as near-perfect copies of their parents? This can be answered in terms of chromosome theory and the genetic code: the fertilized egg which develops into an individual contains a diploid set of chromosomes, half of the set received from each parent, and these chromosomes contain information or a 'programme' which normally ensures that the individual is a copy of the parents.

5·1   Hybrid sterility

Are there genetic mechanisms which allow some individuals to interbreed, and prevent others from doing so? In other words, are there genetic reasons why different species do not hybridize? A variety of such mechanisms is known, leading to failure of interspecific hybrids at various stages.

If an egg is to be fertilized, it must be penetrated by a sperm, and the nuclei of these two cells must fuse. In many cases, sperm of one species is unable to fertilize eggs of another. The mechanism here is usually chemical, the egg secreting a substance which repels foreign sperm, or failing to secrete a substance which attracts them. Such chemical secretions are programmed by the DNA, and so are genetically controlled. If fertilization is successful and a hybrid egg results, half its genetic message will be specifying a creature of one sort, like the father, and half another, like the mother. It is not surprising that most such hybrids die early in development. But where the two sets of information are compatible and a hybrid, such as a mule, reaches maturity, another genetic mechanism comes into play. This is the reduction division, meiosis, in the reproductive cells, where the number of chromosomes is halved in gamete formation. This division cycle begins with the chromosomes associating in pairs, each pair containing one maternal and one paternal chromosome. This pairing is very exact, and involves not just the whole chromosome but sub-units within it, corresponding to sections of DNA. In hybrids, where there are dissimilarities between the two sets of chromosomes, pairing may fail to occur or may be incomplete. The result will be unequal distribution of the genetic material amongst the gametes, some receiving extra chromosomes or parts of chromosomes, and others lacking these. Where the parents have different numbers of chromosomes, meiosis will always be irregular: this is one cause of sterility in mules, for the horse has 64 chromosomes (32 in gametes) and the donkey has 62 (31 in gametes), so a mule has 63 and cannot pair them all off at meiosis.

5·2   Individuals are unique

Are the variations between individuals of a species inherited, or caused by variations in the environment and conditions of life? If they are inherited, what causes them?

This question – the extent to which individual variations are caused by heredity or the environment – is one of the oldest controversies in biology. In order to determine the heritability of some feature, it is necessary to measure the total variability shown within the species, and then, by observation or breeding experiments, to decide how much of that variation is caused by heredity, and how much by different conditions of life. At one extreme are simple features like the different colours of pea flowers and seeds, used in Mendel's experiments, or the human ABO blood-groups, described in the next section, which show no environmental effects, and are entirely determined by heredity. At the other extreme are complex characters like human intelligence, where the two sources of variation are much harder to distinguish. The extent to which individual variations are inherited has been most thoroughly studied in man. Identical twins, which develop from a single fertilized egg and so have the same genetic constitution, provide a good test. Studies of identical twins, especially the rare cases where twins are separated soon after birth and brought up under different circumstances, show that in most traits the greater part (60–100 per cent) of the variation between individuals is inherited. Of course, this is a general rule, not a law: if the wolf that found Romulus and Remus had suckled only one of the twins, the great variation in their potential would have been entirely determined by the environment, not heredity. The continuing controversy over the genetic (inherited) and environmental (éducation) contributions to human intelligence shows how difficult it may be to make an objective estimate of the two components. Estimates of the genetic component of human IQ range from about 20 to 80 per cent, and the argument continues about what is being measured, and how bias is to be avoided. Yet when the heritability of some uncontroversial feature, like bristles in *Drosophila*, is estimated at 80–90 per cent, no one troubles to argue.

The source of much of this heritable variation lies at the molecular level, in the base-sequences of small sections of DNA. Mendel assumed that individuals have a double dose of each hereditary factor, and that these factors might be both the same, as in his true-breeding yellow peas, or might be different, as in yellow peas with mixed green and yellow offspring. In modern terms, this would mean that the segment of DNA controlling the factor in question would either be the same in the chromosome received from each parent, or would differ. This idea, that there are only two alternative forms of a gene (the alternatives are called *alleles*), is an over-simplification. Many, perhaps most, factors have three or more variants within a species, and Mendelian breeding experiments may show that they are all alternative forms of the same section of DNA: this will be so if no individual is found to possess more than two of the possible variants. Such sets of variants – alternative forms of the same part of the chromosome – are called *multiple alleles*.

5·3   Multiple alleles

A simple example of multiple alleles is the human ABO blood-group system, mentioned in section 3·3 as an instance of polymorphism. The ABO blood-groups are controlled by four alleles, symbolized as A_1, A_2, B and O. A and B genes are dominant to O (recessive), A_1 is dominant to A_2, and the two A genes are neither dominant nor recessive to B, so that both alleles are expressed in the phenotype of the AB genotype. The possible genetic constitutions of individuals are A_1A_1, A_1A_2, A_1B, A_1O, A_2A_2, A_2B, A_2O, BB, BO and OO, ten in all. Where there are five alleles, the number of possible genotypes is 15, for six alleles it is 21, and so on. Where a character, such as height or intelligence in human beings, is controlled by many genes, each of which may have several allelic forms, the variety of possible genotypes is very large.

Apart from their interest as a source of variation, multiple alleles introduce another very important idea – that one individual is never an adequate sample of the genes available in a species (Fig. 14). No individual can have more than two alleles of any gene (one in each of a pair of chromosomes), but the species may contain very many sets of multiple alleles.

In general, we may say that the source of the genetic uniqueness of an individual is reshuffling of genes present in the parents. One cause of this shuffling is random segregation or sorting of chromosomes in meiosis: an organism with 20 chromosomes, ten received from each parent, will produce gametes containing ten chromosomes, with every possible assortment of paternal and maternal chromosomes. But in meiosis there

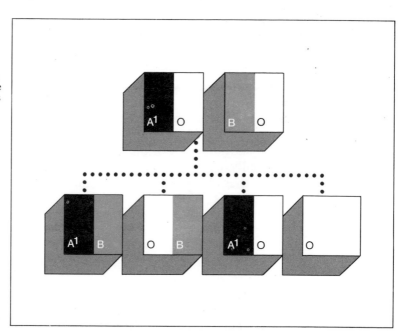

41

is an additional source of variation, omitted, for the sake of simplicity, in the account of this division cycle in section 4·2: this is the phenomenon called *crossing-over*.

5·4   Crossing-over

In the first phase of meiosis, pairs of homologous (one maternal and one paternal) chromosomes associate, and then each chromosome splits into two chromatids, so that there are four associated threads (Fig. 8). A most surprising finding, confirmed by direct observation and by breeding experiments, is that these threads are not tangled like four lengths of string, where the four separate pieces can be recovered by untangling. In meiotic chromosomes the association involves actual breakage and rejoining of the threads, with mutual exchange of sections of chromosome (Fig. 15). Using the string analogy, it is as if one tangled up two pieces of green string and two of white, and on separating them found that a piece of green string was the same length as before but included one or more white sections, while the missing green sections were found to be incorporated in the appropriate places in one of the white pieces. If such a thing happened with string, we would take it to be a miracle or, more probably, a conjuring trick. But with chromosomes in meiosis it is a regular (though not predictable) occurrence.

Besides its other remarkable properties, DNA in early meiosis behaves as if it were easily broken, and as if the loose ends were 'sticky', so that a broken piece of DNA will unite with any other available loose end. The cause seems to be that when two DNA molecules are lying side by side and very close to one another, part of one side chain in each double helix may actually break free from its original partner, and associate with the other molecule. Repair of the breaks will lead to exchange of sections of DNA. So this breakage and rejoining in meiosis results in the exchange or crossing-over of segments, of varying size, between chromosome pairs.

Thus, after meiosis the gametes do not just receive a random mixture of complete paternal and maternal chromosomes; because of crossing-over they receive an assortment of mixed chromosomes, some of them with varying combinations of maternal and paternal segments. These mixing processes will

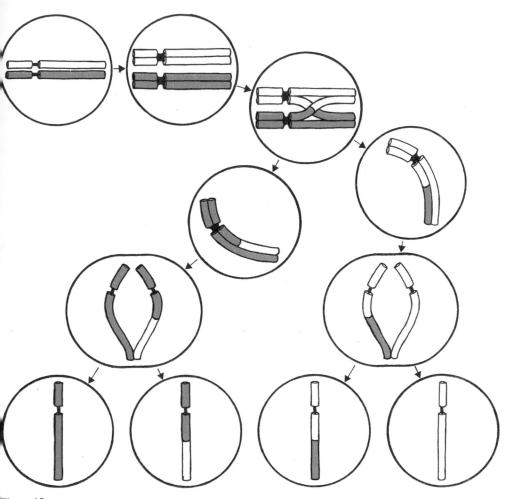

Figure 15
Crossing-over.
Diagrams showing the behaviour of a pair of chromosomes in meiosis (compare with Fig. 8). The example shown is the simplest possible type of crossing-over; two or more cross-overs often occur, when two or more sections of chromosome will be exchanged. If no cross-overs form, the pair of chromosomes will not remain together, and meiosis will be abnormal.

generate an almost infinite variety of gametes, and because every individual is produced by fusion of two gametes, each the result of shuffling of a different set of genes, it would be surprising if the individual genotype were not unique. These reassortments and recombinations, within and between chromosomes, are the source of 'normal' variation between individuals. What might be called 'abnormal' variation has a different cause – *mutation* – which is discussed in the next chapter.

43

6 Mutation

Variation in domesticated animals and plants (section 3·4) shows that the potential variability of a single wild species is enormous, and raises the question of the origin of these variations. New combinations of genes present in wild populations, and especially the occasional appearance, and selection by man, of individuals showing rare recessive traits, may account for much of this variation, but there is another important source, mutation, or the appearance of novelties. In everyday usage, as in science fiction, the words 'mutation' and 'mutant' imply striking and obvious changes, and this was also the original meaning of the terms in genetics. But in the modern molecular theory of genetics, mutation means the occurrence of any change in the genotype, and some known mutations have no detectable effects: they are not manifested in the phenotype. Mutations are of two main sorts. The first, changes in the coding of small sections of DNA, within individual genes, are *point mutations*; the second, large-scale changes in the chromosomes, are *chromosome mutations*.

6·1   Point mutations

With knowledge of the code in which the genetic message is 'written', theoretical understanding of point mutations is fairly simple. Imagine a short section of DNA, within a gene specifying an enzyme, in which the code (symbolized by the initials of the four bases; see Fig. 11) reads:

If the first symbol in this series happens to be the first of a triplet, these bases will be a sequence of four triplets. After transcription and translation by the messenger and transfer RNA system, they will specify the amino acids valine, isoleucine, leucine, and a stop sign. Suppose that by some accident in replication the first base-pair in this section of DNA were to be eliminated. The message now reads:

The first triplet has become ATT, a stop sign, so the remainder will not be translated and the enzyme molecule will lack its last three amino acids.

Alternatively, suppose that an extra base, say G, were inserted immediately before the first C in the original sequence. It now reads:

This specifies arginine, asparagine, proline, methionine, and there is no terminal stop sign, so the subsequent DNA will also be translated and added to the enzyme molecule. These two types of mutation, *deletion* (of one or more bases) and *insertion* (of one or more bases), will clearly have profound effects. But notice that if an insertion or deletion involved three base-pairs, not just one, the effect would be small, adding or deleting a single amino acid in the protein chain.

A commoner type of mutation is a *substitution*, where one base-pair in DNA is replaced by a different one. In the example, suppose the first G in the middle of the sequence were replaced by T, so that the triplet TAG is changed to TAT. Reference to the code shows that both triplets specify isoleucine, so such a mutation would have no effect on the protein, and would not be detectable by any method now available. Most substitutions will alter one amino acid into another at a certain point in the protein chain, and may or may not affect the functioning of that protein. The most drastic substitutions are those changing a triplet specifying an amino acid into a stop sign, or changing a stop sign into an amino acid triplet – the first of these would cut the protein short, and the second would add new amino acids to the end of the chain.

The examples just given are theoretical, but all these types of mutation are found in nature. They are detected at second hand, by determining the sequence of amino acids in proteins taken from different individuals or populations of a species, and looking for variants. The DNA sequence responsible for the normal and variant proteins can be reconstructed by encoding the amino acids in triplets. The best known example of this method is human haemoglobin. The human haemoglobin molecule consists of two pairs of protein chains linked together. The two types of chain, alpha and beta, are each similar in form to the myoglobin molecule shown in Figure 9. The two are specified by genes on different chromosomes. The normal alpha chain contains 141 amino acids, the beta chain 146. By 1973, no less than 169 different mutations in human haemoglobin had been recorded, 62 of them substitutions in the alpha chain, 99 substitutions in the beta chain, one deletion in the alpha chain and seven deletions in the beta. All except one of the 161 substitution mutations can be accounted for by a change in a single base-pair in DNA, the exceptional one requiring two changes. One of the alpha chain substitutions is in the stop triplet, and adds 31 extra amino acids to the chain. The beta chain deletions involve removal of from one to five amino acids. The incidence of these mutations is very variable: some are found to be widely distributed, others are known only from a single family. It is important to notice that each of these mutants is found in children or adults; in other words, none of them inhibits development, and most of them produce no detectable physical symptoms.

The mutations in human haemoglobin are not randomly distributed through the protein chains: some parts of the chain are prone to mutation and others are not. In the beta chain, the 99 known substitution mutations affect 71 out of the 146 amino acids in the chain. The regions showing few or no mutations are the groups which give the molecule its three-dimensional shape; the parts that join the alpha and beta chains together; and the region surrounding the haem group, which carries oxygen. This does not mean that mutations are less likely in these regions, but that most such mutations are lethal, impairing haemoglobin function so seriously that they cause early death. Many lethal mutations of this sort are known in man, experimental animals and plants, and where the precise genetic cause can be elucidated it is usually found to be a point mutation.

About one person in 2000 carries a mutant haemoglobin gene: a few of these are newly arisen within that person, and others have been inherited. The basic cause of these mutations is error in replication of DNA, where the newly-formed DNA molecule is not a perfect copy of the parent molecule. It is important to find out how frequent such mistakes are, in other words, what the *mutation rate* is.

The rate at which mutations appear is greatly increased by treatment with X-rays, and by other radiation such as gamma rays and ultraviolet light. The rate is also increased by various chemicals, including mustard gas and hydrogen peroxide. In nature, the commonest cause of mutation is probably the background radiation to which all organisms are subject, from cosmic rays, natural radioactivity and so on. The natural, or spontaneous, mutation rate has been calculated for a variety of different mutations in animals, plants and micro-organisms. There are two ways of expressing this rate, either as mutations per gene, that is, mutations in the section of DNA that specifies a particular protein, or controls a visible character; or as mutations per base-pair in the DNA. The spontaneous mutation rate per gene, calculated for mutations with a visible effect, not for 'hidden' ones like those haemoglobin mutations which produce no physical symptoms, is about one in 100 000 per generation, for a wide variety of organisms. Each gene contains a large number of DNA base-pairs: for example, the genes coding haemoglobin chains, with about 150 amino acids, contain about 450 base-pairs, since each amino acid is coded by three base-pairs. The mutation rate per base-pair is therefore much lower than the gene rate, and a base-pair rate of about one in 10 million per generation is generally accepted. If this rate is constant, as it seems to be, it means that 'long' genes, specifying long protein chains (some contain 600 amino acids) will have a higher mutation rate than 'short' genes.

Because a mutation may occur whenever DNA replicates, and since cell division, which involves DNA replication, is going on all the time in our bodies, we are accumulating mutations throughout life. Mutations are rare events, but our bodies contain so many dividing cells that every human being probably carries between 10 and 100 base-pair mutations that have arisen during his or her life.

6·2   Chromosome mutations

The point mutations just discussed usually involve changes in single base-pairs in DNA – they are very small-scale phenomena. Chromosome mutations involve changes in large pieces of DNA, segments of chromosomes or even whole chromosomes. And while point mutations imply actual change in the genetic material, chromosome mutations usually rearrange existing material. Chromosome mutations can be provoked by the same agents as point mutations – radiation and chemicals – but also occur spontaneously. Point mutations occur when DNA reproduces itself, and chromosome mutations

47

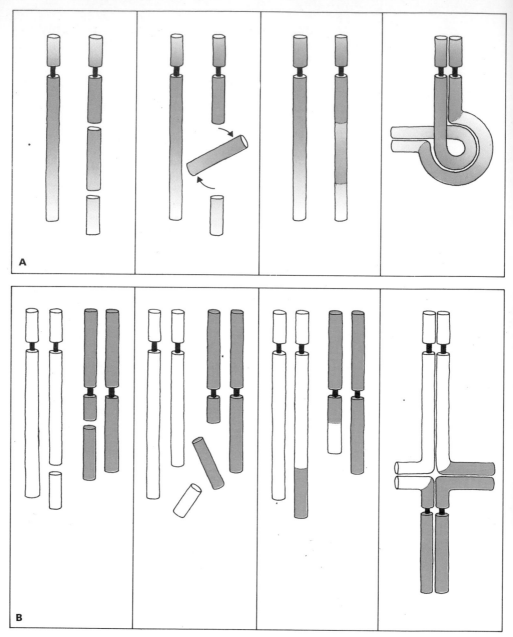

Figure 16
Chromosome mutations.
A, inversion. A pair of homologous chromosomes is shown. One breaks in two places, and is 'mended' with the middle segment inverted. The last diagram shows how inversions can be recognized when the chromosomes pair off in meiosis: matching parts can only pair exactly if the inverted segment forms a loop. B, translocation. Two pairs of chromosomes are shown. One of each breaks, and is 'mended' with the wrong segment. In meiosis, matching parts can only pair off if the four chromosomes associate in a cross, as in the last diagram.

occur when the nucleus reproduces itself in cell division, especially in meiosis.

In section 5·4, crossing-over was described, a peculiarity of the meiotic cycle which results in exchange of sections between homologous chromosomes: DNA behaves as if it were easily broken, and as if the loose ends were sticky. Chromosome mutations are mostly due to errors or mis-pairings in crossing-over. They are of six main types: (i) *inversions*, where a section of a chromosome maintains its position, but is turned round end to end (Fig. 16A); (ii) *translocations*, where sections of chromosome are exchanged between non-homologous chromosomes, not between homologues, as in normal crossing-over (Fig. 16B); (iii) and (iv) *deletions* and *duplications*, which arise when crossing-over is unequal, one chromosome of the pair receiving more than 'it loses, so that a part of it is duplicated, while its partner has a part deleted; (v) *fusions*, where two whole or almost whole chromosomes join end to end, reducing the number of separate chromosomes by one; and (vi) *unequal divisions*, where after a cycle of cell division one of the two daughter nuclei receives one or more extra chromosomes, and the other lacks one or more.

Examples of all these types of chromosome mutation are found. Inversions and translocations are the commonest types. They can often be recognized under the microscope, by the pattern of banding of the chromosomes, or by unusual pairing patterns in cells undergoing meiosis (Fig. 16). In our own species, to take one example, 3 per cent of the population of Edinburgh, Scotland, carry an inversion of part of chromosome 1, while the standard human set of chromosomes differs from that of chimpanzees by six inversions, and from gorilla by eight. In meiosis, inversions form loops (Fig. 16A) and translocations form crosses (Fig. 16B), and these complications often lead to gametes that lack segments of chromosomes, and so to reduced fertility. Inversions and translocations are therefore genetic changes which may prevent hybridization between different species. But in many animal species, inversions are so widespread that they are clearly not harmful, and in the fruit-fly *Drosophila*, the frequency of different inversion patterns varies with the seasons, in an annual cycle that seems to be maintained by natural selection. The explanation may be that the inverted segments act as 'super-genes', for the looping in meiosis means that crossing-over within the inversion is unlikely, so that a block of genes can be kept together.

Deletions and duplications also turn up in laboratory organisms. Deletions, causing lack of chromosome segments, are frequently lethal. Duplications, on the other hand, may be an important source of evolutionary innovations (see section 11·3). Fusions and unequal divisions seem to have played an important part in evolution, otherwise it is hard to see why different species have different numbers of chromosomes. For example, the difference between a donkey, with a diploid set of 62 chromosomes, and a horse, with 64, or between a man, with 46, and a gorilla or chimpanzee, with 48, is most probably due to some past event of fusion in the donkey and human lines. An example in species of *Drosophila* is shown in Figure 17. Fusion may make little difference to the genotype, since it involves no gain or loss of material, but unequal division, producing cells lacking or with extra chromosomes, is much more drastic. Lack of a chromosome is usually lethal, as might be expected, but extra chromosomes also produce serious disturbances. In man, one or two children in every thousand are afflicted by mongolism, a malfunction in which the face has a characteristic cast, mental development is retarded, males are sterile and females very infertile. This is caused by an extra chromosome, matching one of pair 21 in the standard set (Fig. 7), so that a mongol has 47 chromosomes, with three number 21s.

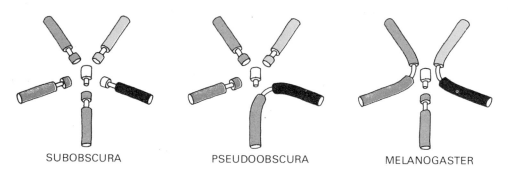

SUBOBSCURA   PSEUDOOBSCURA   MELANOGASTER

Figure 17
Chromosome fusions in the fruit-fly *Drosophila*. The diagrams show the chromosomes of haploid cells (gametes). *Drosophila subobscura* has one dot-like and five rod-like chromosomes. The pattern found in *D. pseudoobscura* can be derived by fusion between two chromosomes, and that of *D. melanogaster* by two such fusions.

6·3   Polyploidy

The most extreme examples of unequal cell division are those in which the chromosome number is doubled. This will occur if division of the chromosomes is not followed by division of the nucleus. The normal number of chromosomes for a species is the diploid number, while the half-set found in gametes is haploid. Doubling of the diploid set produces cells with a tetraploid complement (Greek *tetra* = four), and a cross between a diploid organism (with haploid gametes) and a tetraploid (with diploid gametes) would produce a triploid, with three times the haploid number. Organisms with chromosome numbers which are some multiple of a basic set are called polyploids. Polyploidy is uncommon in animals, but it has been of great importance in plant evolution: almost half the known species of flowering plants are polyploids.

Suppose that in a plant, an abnormal cell division in a developing bud or flower produces a cell with double the normal number of chromosomes. This cell may continue to divide, and all its descendants will also have a double set of chromosomes. In this way, a tetraploid flower or branch may develop and produce pollen and egg-cells that are diploid, not haploid, as is usual. Self-fertilization of these flowers could then produce a batch of tetraploid seeds. Such events are improbable in normal plants, because meiosis, the reduction division in the male and female parts of the flower, will be disturbed in the tetraploid cells, since the chromosomes will tend to associate in fours, not pairs. This will lead to irregular chromosome numbers in the gametes, and to reduced fertility. But suppose the plant were a hybrid between two different species, one with a diploid number of (say) eight, the other with twelve. Such a hybrid would have ten chromosomes, four from one parent and six from the other, and would be completely sterile, because the chromosomes cannot pair off at meiosis. But if a tetraploid flower arose in this hybrid plant, as outlined above, it would be fertile, since in meiosis the twenty chromosomes would fall into ten homologous pairs. These flowers, if self-fertilized, will produce seeds combining the genotypes of the two parent species. What is more, the plants growing from these seeds will be interfertile, so forming the basis of a reproductive community, but will not form fertile hybrids with either of the parent species. By this sort of accident, an entirely new species of plant can arise more or less instantaneously.

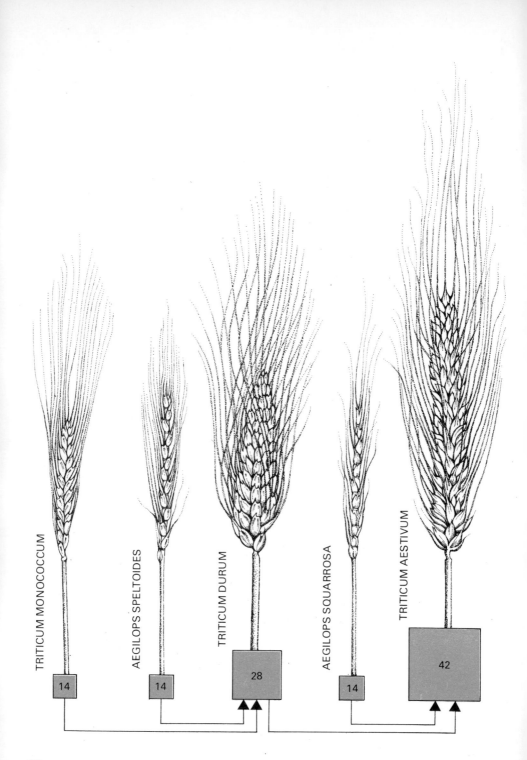

TRITICUM MONOCOCCUM

AEGILOPS SPELTOIDES

TRITICUM DURUM

AEGILOPS SQUARROSA

TRITICUM AESTIVUM

14

14

28

14

42

Polyploids can be produced quite readily in the laboratory, by treating plants with colchicine, a substance extracted from *Colchicum*, the autumn crocus. Colchicine interferes with cell division so that the chromosomes divide but the nucleus does not. Polyploid plants are found to differ from diploids in having larger cells (because the nucleus is larger), thicker, fleshier leaves, and larger flowers and fruit. Fleshier leaves and larger fruit are, of course, highly desirable features in plants cultivated for food, and it is not surprising that many of our staple food plants are polyploids. Perhaps the most important example is wheat (Fig. 18). The wheat first cultivated by early man was a diploid species, *Triticum monococcum* or einkorn wheat, with 14 chromosomes, still found wild in the Near East. *Triticum durum*, the hard or 'macaroni' wheat now cultivated for pasta, is a tetraploid species, with 28 chromosomes. It arose by chromosome doubling in a hybrid between einkorn wheat and a grass, *Aegilops speltoides*, also with 14 chromosomes, which grows as a weed in fields in the Near East. This tetraploid wheat may have been found wild by man, or may have first appeared, and been selected, in some early wheat field. The wheat now grown for bread, *Triticum aestivum*, is a hexaploid (Greek *hexa* = six) species, with 42 chromosomes, which arose by a second episode of chromosome doubling in a hybrid between durum wheat, with 28 chromosomes, and another grass, *Aegilops squarrosa*, with 14 chromosomes. Durum and bread wheats have been 'recreated' in the laboratory, by inducing chromosome doubling with colchicine in hybrids between the three wild species.

Many other cultivated plants are polyploids, and the production of new varieties with increased yields by inducing chromosome doubling is an important branch of agricultural research.

In plants, new species can arise instantaneously by chromosome doubling, and new species can be 'created' in the laboratory. But this process alone will not explain evolution, for polyploid species are rare in animals. This is not because the nuclear accidents causing chromosome doubling do not happen in animals: examination of the chromosomes of 227 human embryos which died before birth showed that two of them were tetraploids, and in many animals, especially insects, certain organs of the body are always formed by polyploid cells, in which nuclear division has stopped but chromosome division continues. The main reason why polyploid species are

Figure 18
Polyploidy and the history of wheat. The diagram shows how bread wheat, *Triticum aestivum*, has evolved, by successive chromosome doubling in hybrids between different species.

rare in animals is that most animals are not hermaphrodites capable of self-fertilization, and self-fertilization, common in plants, is necessary for successful species-formation by polyploidy. The only animal groups in which polyploid species are frequent are various hermaphrodite worms, and some crustaceans, insects and a few other animals that reproduce asexually, the eggs developing without fertilization. Yet there are polyploid species and groups of species in some sexual animals – certain frogs and fishes, for example. Occasional chromosome doubling in the history of animals is one way of explaining the thousandfold increase in DNA content of the nucleus which has taken place in evolution (Fig. 19).

Figure 19
The amount of DNA in organisms. The scale is logarithmic, each line representing a tenfold increase over the one above. The amount recorded is the haploid content per cell (half the content of a single cell in diploid organisms like ourselves), measured in picograms. One picogram of DNA contains about 900 million base-pairs. The height of the four curves has no particular significance, and in fact the third group contains more species than the other three put together.

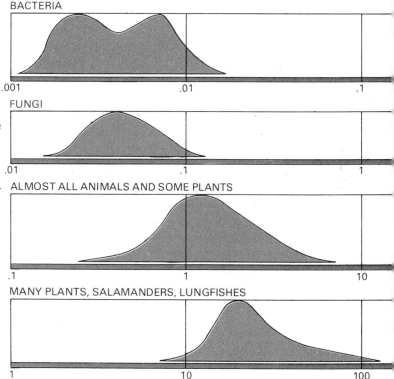

In this chapter, three types of mutation have been described, polyploidy, chromosome mutations and point mutations. Mutations are due to imperfect copying of DNA, in replication, or to imperfect chromosome separation, in nuclear division. All mutations are therefore accidental, and like all accidents, their incidence is random, and subject to chance.

Polyploidy – doubling of chromosome number – is an important means of species formation in plants, but is rare in animals. The various kinds of chromosome mutation lead to rearrangements of the genetic material, and have varying effects, ranging from lethal to undetectable. They are an important cause of sterility in hybrids between species, tending to keep existing species distinct, and one class of chromosome mutations – duplication – is a source of evolutionary novelty (section 11·3). Point mutations, changing single 'letters' in the genetic code, are probably the commonest type of mutation, and lead to the production of many variant genes within a species. This situation recalls polymorphism, discussed in section 3·3, and the multiple alleles discussed in section 5·3, where members of a species may carry one of several variant genes at the same point on the chromosome. But to take the next step in the argument, and assume that point mutations are the cause of multiple alleles, is to make a guess about the past: that mutations arising in earlier members of the species have become widespread. This idea, of changes in gene frequency through time, introduces *natural selection*, which is discussed in the next two chapters.

7 Natural selection theory

Natural Selection is at the same time the explanation of every-thing and nothing in the Darwinian theory of evolution ... In all my life, I never have met a text which offers so many diffi-culties of all sorts as The Origin of Species.
Leon Croizat, *Space, Time, Form: the Biological Synthesis,*
1962

Natural selection – 'the struggle for existence', 'the preserva-tion of favoured races', 'the survival of the fittest' – was the central idea of Darwin's theory of evolution. Darwin based his case on the discrepancy between the actual and potential offspring of an organism* (or a pair of organisms in sexual species), on the vast destruction of gametes and young in-dividuals entailed by this discrepancy, on the idea that some variations might be advantageous and others harmful, and on analogy with artificial selection, by man, in domesticated ani-mals and plants. Since Darwin's work, the lapse of time has been sufficient for many examples of natural selection to have been observed, in nature and in laboratory experiments, and knowledge of genetics has given selection theory a sound basis. Unfortunately, selection theory (or theoretical population genetics) is now one of the most sophisticated and mathemati-cal branches of biology, difficult to summarize or discuss in simple terms. It is fair to say that when he introduced natural selection, Darwin did not fully appreciate the subtlety of his idea. Natural selection may have appeared to the Victorians as a blunt instrument ('nature red in tooth and claw', in Tenny-son's pre-Darwinian phrase), but in the modern theory it is an agent of remarkable refinement and variety, and some of those ideas must be introduced here, if only to give an idea of the complications that arise in understanding or explaining real situations.

*The example Darwin gave was not an obvious one like the female cod, capable of laying three or four million eggs in a year, but the slowest breeder of all, the elephant. Darwin calculated that the offspring of a single pair of elephants could number at least 15 million after 500 years.

In this chapter, a theoretical example of selection is discussed, to bring in some aspects of population genetics, and in chapter 8 there are instances of selection in action.

Suppose that a new point mutation, involving a change in a single base-pair in DNA (a 'letter' of the genetic code), has appeared in one individual of a sexually reproducing species. What will be the fate of this mutant molecule? This depends first on where (i.e. in what cell) the mutation arises. If it is in a cell of the body, no matter whether its effects are large or small, the mutation dies with that individual and is lost. But if it arises in a reproductive cell (sperm, egg), or in a cell which will give rise to some or all* of the reproductive cells, there is a possibility that the mutation will be passed on to the next generation. If this is so, the mutant gene becomes interesting, and we can ask what its effects are.

*Even if the mutation arises in that embryonic cell which will, by subsequent division, give rise to *all* the gametes of the organism, the mutant DNA will only be present in half the gametes, and will, on average, be transmitted to half the offspring. This is because the mutation will be in one chromosome of a homologous pair, and in meiosis, the reduction division which allots half the diploid set of chromosomes to each gamete, half the gametes will receive the mutation-bearing chromosome, and half the normal one.

There are three possibilities: that the effects are harmful, that they are neutral, or that they are beneficial. In reality, most point mutations will change the coding for one sub-unit of a protein molecule (section 6·1), and may affect the functioning of that molecule. Many such changes will be for the worse, while some (like a large proportion of the known point mutations in human haemoglobin) will have no obvious effect, and a few may improve the functioning. It is easy to think of beneficial mutations in science fiction terms – wings sprouting from a mammal, or eyes appearing in the back of a man's head – but most beneficial mutations will be on a very mundane level, perhaps allowing a chemical reaction to proceed slightly faster, or at a slightly lower temperature.

Later we shall consider the fate of each of these three types of mutation – harmful, neutral and beneficial – but first it is necessary to ask how we might recognize these classes of mutation. It should be evident that this can only be done by comparing the performance or success of the organisms carrying them with those carrying the normal, non-mutant (or 'wild-type') gene. And success here will mean reproductive success, the efficiency with which the gene is transmitted to subsequent generations. The main point is that the status of a mutation, whether it is advantageous, neutral or harmful, is something that can only be assessed by observing the success of individuals carrying it, preferably over several generations. Instead of 'success', it is customary to use the Darwinian term '*fitness*' (adaptive value is a synonym), and to attach a numerical value to it. Such a value – an estimate of the fitness of a genotype – will be relative, because one can only compare the fitness of one genotype with that of another, and in a particular environment.

Fitness in this technical sense is defined as an estimate of the contribution that a particular genotype will make to the next generation, expressed as a proportion of the gametes contributing to that generation. Imagine that in a breeding population of a species we found that a certain gene was represented in two alternative forms (alleles), symbolized by 'A' and 'a', and the proportion of genotypes was 25% AA, 50% Aa and 25% aa (Fig. 20). The proportion of each of the two alleles here is 50% ($25+\frac{1}{2} \times 50$). This will also be the ratio of the gametes that combined to produce this population and we would expect the same proportions in the next generation. But suppose that in the next generation we found that the genotypes were 36% AA, 48% Aa and 16% aa. The proportions of the two alleles are now 60% 'A' ($36+\frac{1}{2} \times 48$) and 40% 'a' ($16+\frac{1}{2} \times 48$): the 'A' gene has been transmitted more efficiently than 'a' (whose effects are obviously relatively defective at some stage in the life cycle), and for every 100 'A' gametes contributing to the first generation, there are 120 contributing to the second, while for every 100 'a' gametes in the first generation there are only 80 in the second. The relative fitness of the two genotypes can be expressed by the ratio between these two numbers: for 'A' it is $\frac{120}{100}$ or 1·2, and for 'a' $\frac{80}{100}$ or 0·8. The mean fitness of the population is

$$\frac{1·2+0·8}{2},$$

or 1.0, and will always have that value.

The *selection coefficient* is defined as 1 − fitness, and in this example for 'a' it will be $1 - 0·8 = 0·2$, and for 'A' it is $1 - 1·2 = -0·2$. A positive selection coefficient means that a gene is decreasing in frequency in successive generations, and is relatively harmful, while a negative selection coefficient means that a gene is beneficial, and will increase in successive generations.

We can now return to the example of a new mutation, and consider first what will happen if it is harmful.

7·1   Harmful mutations

We have assumed that a harmful mutation appears in the reproductive cells of one individual of a population, let us say

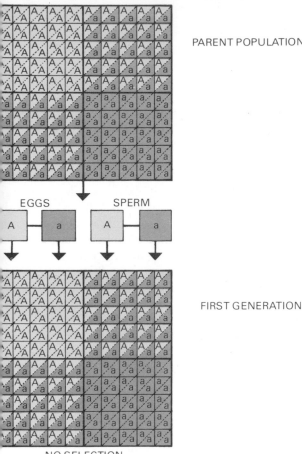

PARENT POPULATION

FIRST GENERATION

NO SELECTION

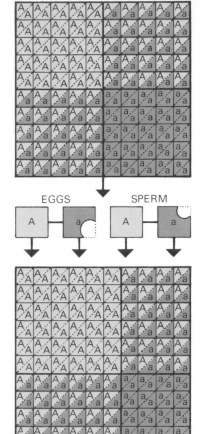

SELECTION AGAINST a

Figure 20
How natural selection is recognized.
The blocks of squares represent populations of
organisms, and each small square is an individual.
A single gene with two alternative alleles (A and a)
is considered. On the left, the two alleles are found
in the same proportion in the parent and
descendent populations: the alleles are equally
successful, and there is no selection. On the right,
the allele 'a' is less common in the descendent
population, and this is interpreted as being due to
selection against the gametes carrying 'a'.

in a male. Some of the sperm produced by this individual will
then carry the mutant DNA molecule, and some of these may
fertilize eggs produced by one or more females which will lack
the mutation, having the normal or 'wild-type' gene in its
place. The resulting fertilized eggs, and the individuals that develop from them, will then be *heterozygous* for the mutation,
carrying the mutant in one chromosome of a pair (derived
from the father), and the normal gene in the maternal member
of the pair. Whether the mutation produces any effect in
these heterozygous individuals will then depend on whether
it is dominant or recessive. A dominant mutant will affect the

59

organism (the phenotype) in heterozygotes. A recessive one will only be manifested in *homozygotes*, where there is a Mendelian double-dose of the gene (see section 4.1), that is, it is the same in both chromosomes of the pair. Homozygous individuals can only be produced by mating between parents which are both carriers of the gene, so there can be no individuals homozygous for the new mutation until it is sufficiently widespread for two carriers to mate.

We do not yet know why some genes are expressed in a single dose (dominant), why some are only expressed in homozygotes (recessive), or why some pairs of genes (alleles) are both active (incomplete dominance), but we do know that these terms are relative (p. 37), depending on whether the visible effects or the protein product of the gene are considered. Nor can we predict whether a new mutation will be dominant, recessive, or incompletely dominant, in which case the organism will show the effects of both the normal and mutant genes. It is an observed fact that most mutations are harmful and recessive, but it does not follow that new mutations will also be recessive, for it is very likely that the mutations observed (in *Drosophila* or human beings, for example) are not new, but have appeared millions of times before in previous generations, and that selection has adjusted the dominant/recessive mechanism so that the mutation does least damage, and is recessive. We do know that the dominant or recessive status of a particular gene is not fixed for all time, but can be changed by modifying genes. We also know that in *Drosophila*, for example, whenever there is a variety of mutant forms of a particular gene, these mutants show incomplete dominance to one another, but are recessive to the wild-type or normal gene. The most reasonable assumption is that new mutations will be neither recessive nor dominant, but incompletely dominant, manifesting some effect in heterozygotes.

Returning to the example, the fate of a harmful mutation will certainly be influenced by which of the three categories, dominant, recessive or incompletely dominant, it falls into. If the mutant is dominant, its effects will be fully expressed in the next generation; if partially dominant it will have some immediate effect in this generation; and if recessive it will not be expressed at all in this heterozygous generation. The fate of the mutation will also depend on how harmful it is, or, in population genetic terms, what its fitness is (p. 58). A dominant lethal mutation, killing all carriers early in life, before they can reproduce, will disappear immediately, and will have fitness zero, and a selection coefficient (1 − fitness) of one. A less harmful mutation might have a much greater fitness, perhaps 0·95, and a selection coefficient of 0·05: this would mean that if 100 individuals carried the mutation in one generation, there would be only 95 in the next. But it must be emphasized that all such numbers are statistical or probabilistic estimates and can only be calculated for large populations, where the genes in question are represented in such large numbers that fluctuations due to chance can be neglected. In a particular situation these numbers no more predict the outcome than a bookmaker's odds predict the order in which the horses will pass the post. In our example, where a new mutation has appeared in a single individual and been transmitted to a few progeny, it is quite possible that a predator will eat all the offspring at once, and the mutation will be lost. But neglecting such accidents, the probability of a mutation being transmitted to subsequent generations can be calculated, and it turns out that whenever the gene confers some disadvantage (the selection coefficient is positive), it will eventually be eliminated. A dominant mutant, expressed in all its carriers, will be eliminated rapidly. An incompletely dominant gene, partially expressed in heterozygotes and fully expressed in homozygotes, will be eliminated more slowly. And a recessive gene, only expressed in homozygotes, will be eliminated very slowly indeed, for selection cannot act on it until it has become sufficiently widespread for matings between heterozygotes to occur, since homozygotes are produced only from matings between parents who both carry the gene. Figure 21 shows a well-known example of the elimination of a harmful mutation, one that is unusual because it is recessive in females and dominant in males.

Some idea of these different rates of elimination comes from calculations of the 'force' tending to eliminate a disadvantageous gene from a population: this can be thought of as the number of generations necessary to reduce the frequency of the gene by a certain amount. For example, we can compare a recessive gene which confers a 1 per cent disadvantage (in homozygotes) with an incompletely dominant gene with a 1 per cent disadvantage in heterozygotes and a 2 per cent disadvantage in homozygotes. If we imagine that these genes have become widespread in a population, to reduce the number of

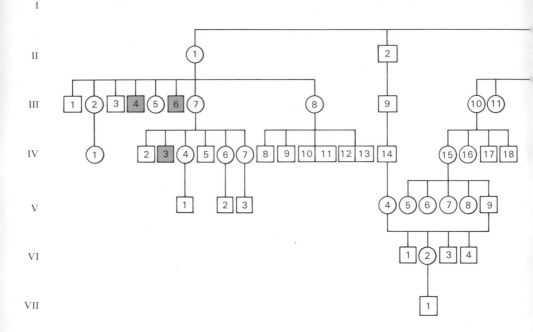

I

1 Queen Victoria 1819–1901

II

1 Victoria 1840–1901
2 Edward VII 1841–1910
3 Alice 1843–1878
4 Alfred 1844–1900
5 Helena 1846–1923
6 Louise 1848–1939
7 Arthur 1850–1942
8 Leopold 1853–1884
9 Beatrice 1857–1944

III

1 William II (Kaiser) 1859–1941
2 Charlotte 1860–1919
3 Henry 1862–1929
4 Sigismund 1864–1866
5 Victoria 1866–1929
6 Waldemar 1868–1879
7 Sophie 1870–1932
8 Margaret 1872–1954

9 George V 1865–1936

10 Victoria 1863–1950
11 Elizabeth 1864–1918
12 Irene 1866–1953
13 Ernest 1868–1937
14 Frederick 1870–1873
15 Alexandra 1872–1918
16 Maria 1874–1878

17 Christian 1867–1900
18 Albert 1869–1931
19 Helena 1870–1948
20 Marie Louise 1870–1956
21 Frederick b. & d. 1876

22 Alice b. 1883
23 Charles 1884–1954

24 Alexander 1886–1960
25 Victoria Eugenie 1887–1969
26 Leopold 1889–1922
27 Maurice 1891–1914

IV

1 Feodora 1879–1945

2 George 1890–1947
3 Alexander 1893–1920
4 Helen b. 1896

5 Paul 1901–1964
6 Irene b. 1904
7 Katherine b. 1913
8 Frederick 1893–1916
9 Maximilian 1894–1914
10 Philip 1896–1944
11 Wolfgang b. 1896
12 Richard b. 1901
13 Christopher 1901–1943

14 George VI 1895–1952

15 Alice 1885–1969
16 Louise 1889–1965
17 George 1892–1938
18 Louis b. 1900

19 Waldemar 1889–1945
20 Sigismund b. 1896
21 Henry 1900–1904

22 Olga 1895–1918
23 Titania 1897–1918
24 Maria 1899–1918
25 Anastasia 1901–1918
26 Alexis 1904–1918

27 May b. 1906
28 Rupert 1907–1928

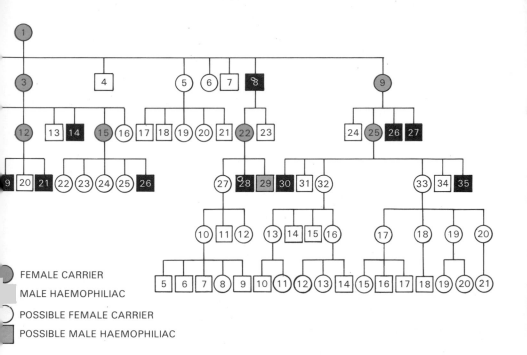

FEMALE CARRIER

MALE HAEMOPHILIAC

POSSIBLE FEMALE CARRIER

POSSIBLE MALE HAEMOPHILIAC

29 Maurice b. & d. 1910

30 Alfonso 1907–1938
31 Jaime b. 1908
32 Beatrice b. 1909
33 Maria b. 1911
34 Juan b. 1913
35 Gonzalo 1914–1934

V

1 Michael b. 1921

2 Amadeo b. 1943
3 Richard b. 1948

4 Elizabeth II b. 1926

5 Margarita b. 1905
6 Theodora 1906–1969
7 Cecilie 1911–1937
8 Sophie b. 1914
9 Philip b. 1921

10 Anne b. 1932
11 Richard b. 1933
12 Elizabeth b. 1936

13 Sandra b. 1936

14 Marco b. 1937
15 Marino b. 1939
16 Olympia b. 1943

17 Victoria b. 1941
18 Giovanna b. 1943
19 Maria Theresa b. 1945
20 Anna b. 1948

VI

1 Charles b. 1948
2 Anne b. 1950
3 Andrew b. 1960
4 Edward b. 1964

5 Ian b. 1959
6 Charles b. 1960
7 Simon b. 1962
8 Alice b. 1965
9 Malcolm b. 1967

10 Alessandro b. 1960
11 Desideria b. 1962

12 Aliki b. 1967
13 Sybilla b. 1968
14 Paul b. 1970

15 Victoria b. 1961
16 Francisco b. 1964
17 Marco b. 1965

18 Alfonso b. 1969

19 Cristina b. 1968
20 Isabel b. 1970

21 Astrid b. 1972

VII

1 Peter b. 1977

Figure 21
Haemophilia in the descendants
of Queen Victoria.
Haemophilia is due to a
mutation in one of the genes
producing the proteins that
cause clotting of the blood.
Haemophiliacs or 'bleeders' are
at risk because they may bleed
to death from trivial accidents.

Haemophilia shows a peculiar pattern of inheritance, called sex-linked, because the gene is on the X chromosome (cf. Fig. 7). The gene is recessive, and has no effect in females (XX), except in the very rare cases where both parents carry the mutation. In males (XY), the mutation behaves as if it were dominant, since there is only one X chromosome, one copy of the gene, and no 'wild-type' gene to mask its effects. Queen Victoria carried a newly-arisen haemophilia mutant on one of her X chromosomes. Half of her children would be expected to carry the mutation, but only the male carriers would be haemophiliacs. In fact, two of her five daughters were definite carriers; her eldest daughter, Victoria, may have been a carrier; and there is no way of telling whether Louise, who died without offspring, was affected. Only one of her four sons, Leopold, was affected. Although frequently ill with internal bleeding, he lived 31 years before dying from a brain haemorrhage, and had two children, a son who was unaffected and a daughter who was a carrier (daughters of haemophiliacs are always carriers, for they must have the father's X chromosome). The daughter is Princess Alice, the only surviving granddaughter of Queen Victoria, and probably the only surviving carrier of the mutant gene. She is shown here

at the christening of Princess Anne's son in December 1977: Princess Anne's family, descended through Queen Victoria's eldest son, is free of the mutation.

Queen Victoria's granddaughter Alexandra (III 15) married Tsar Nicholas II and introduced haemophilia into the Russian royal family. Her son, the Tsarevitch, was haemophiliac and her four daughters may have included carriers, but this branch became extinct when the family was assassinated in the Russian revolution. Through Queen Victoria's youngest daughter the mutation was introduced into the Spanish royal family, but it is probably now extinct there. Through Queen Victoria's eldest daughter the mutation may have been introduced into the German royal family (III 4, 6, 7), but it is now extinct there.

This example gives some idea of the difficulties in accurate genetic analysis extended over several generations. Even in genealogies as well known as those of European royalty there are many unanswerable questions, especially with a trait like haemophilia, where female carriers are only identifiable if they have affected male descendants. Yet it is often impossible to establish the cause of deaths in infancy a century ago (e.g. III 4, III 6).

carriers of the incompletely dominant gene from one individual in a hundred to one in a thousand will require about 230 generations, and the same number of generations will reduce the frequency from one in a thousand to one in ten thousand. But for the recessive gene, it will take about 90 000 generations to reduce carriers from one in a hundred to one in a thousand, and 900 000 generations to reduce it from one in a thousand to one in ten thousand.

The reason for this enormous difference is that natural selection acts on individual organisms, eliminating inefficient phenotypes. But what is selected, and allowed to pass from generation to generation, is not phenotypes but genotypes. Recessive genes, not expressed in the phenotype of heterozygotes, are to a large extent shielded from natural selection, especially if they are rare. This is because homozygous individuals, in whom the characteristic is expressed, have to receive the gene from both parents and will be very uncommon. Even if a recessive mutation is lethal, and kills all homozygotes early in life, it will take about 900 generations to reduce its frequency from one in a hundred to one in a thousand of the population. This may seem to be useless knowledge, but it can have practical consequences. There are many different lethal and sub-lethal recessive mutations in the human population. It seems obvious that it would be a good idea to try to identify carriers (heterozygotes) of these genes, and to discourage marriages between them, so avoiding the birth of afflicted homozygotes. But the result of such a policy would actually be to increase the frequency of these harmful genes, because they can only be reduced in number by the birth, and selective elimination, of homozygotes; or by preventing carriers from breeding at all.

Summarizing this section, natural selection will eliminate harmful mutations from a population at a rate which varies with the harmfulness of the mutation (the lack of fitness of its carriers), and with its degree of dominance. This type of selection, eliminating variants, tends to maintain a species unchanged, and is called *stabilizing* selection.

7·2   Neutral mutations

If a neutral mutation, having no selective advantage or disadvantage, appears in one member of a population, the number of individuals carrying it in subsequent generations will increase or decrease entirely by chance. Once again, the probability of various outcomes can be calculated, but here the analogy with a bookmaker's odds or a roulette wheel is more obvious. In a large population, the chances are about two to one that the new mutant gene will survive into the next generation, about six to one that it will have disappeared by the tenth generation, about fifty to one that it will be gone by the hundredth generation, and there is only one chance in a thousand that it will persist for a thousand generations.

These are probabilities, not predictions, and over long periods of time thousands of neutral mutations might appear in a population, and purely by chance one or two may increase in number sufficiently to become widespread or even universal (Fig. 22).

These probabilities apply in large populations, but increase in gene frequency by chance fluctuations is much more likely

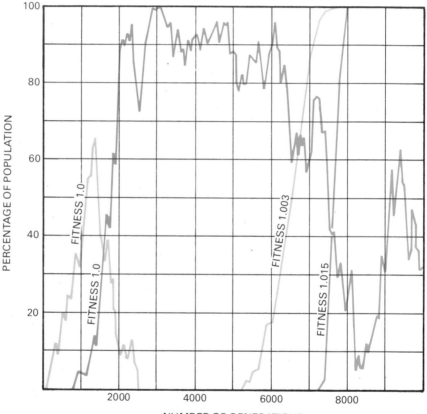

Figure 22
Computer simulations of the fate of new mutations.
Because we can hardly ever observe new mutations, or their fate in the wild, computer simulations are the only way of visualizing the effects of selection and of chance. The graph shows selected results when neutral (fitness = 1·0) and advantageous (fitness more than one) mutations were simulated. The first mutation in the trial is neutral. It becomes widespread, but then fades

away and becomes extinct. The second is also neutral. It almost succeeds in becoming fixed (present in every individual), but continues to fluctuate and is present in about a third of the population at the end of the trial. The third and fourth mutations are advantageous. The third one gives a very slight advantage (three in a thousand), and becomes fixed after about 2000 generations. The fourth has greater fitness, and is fixed after 700 generations.

in small populations. To take the most extreme example, if the mutation arises in one member of a population of only two, such as Adam and Eve, the odds that it will be transmitted to half the next generation are even, and once a gene is present in half the population it is well on the way to being 'fixed', or present in all members. In nature, population bottlenecks like this, when a species or breeding population is reduced to only two members and then recovers, are extremely unlikely. But in a breeding population of a hundred the chance of neutral mutations becoming fixed is far higher than in large populations: the average number of generations required to fix a gene by chance is four times the effective breeding population, 400 generations for a population of a hundred, 4000 for one of a thousand. This process, the chance fixation of a neutral (or even disadvantageous) mutation in small populations, is called *genetic drift*.

From experiments with the fly *Drosophila* it has been established that genetic drift can cause slightly disadvantageous mutations to be fixed in small populations, against the pressure of selection. But whether genetic drift plays an important part in evolution is controversial.

This is partly because of the impossibility of recognizing neutral genes or their effects. The fact that some attribute of an organism appears useless to us is no guarantee that it is so. Investigation of apparently useless features has shown that some do, after all, have survival value. And while it may be possible to show that a certain feature has survival value, and is subject to selection, it is never possible to show that a feature has no such value, and is selectively neutral: we may not have looked carefully or closely enough.

Because of the nature of the genetic code, neutral mutations surely occur. Any change in a 'letter' of the code (i.e. a base-pair in DNA) is a mutation, but since the code is redundant, with some amino acids coded by several different triplets, many such changes will not alter the amino acid specified (for example, changing 'TAG' to 'TAT' – see p. 45), will not be detectable, and may* be neutral. But no mutation that is expressed in the phenotype, causing some small difference in the constitution of the organism carrying it, can safely be regarded as neutral, with no selective advantage or disadvantage whatever.

*I write 'may' rather than 'must' because a different triplet, though coding the same amino acid, might require a different transfer RNA, perhaps a less abundant one, and so be disadvantageous.

In the early days of genetics, before the nature of the hereditary material was known, it was easy to think of superficial features of organisms as direct expressions of single genes. Thus in Mendel's experiments, described in section 4·1, one might imagine a 'gene for wrinkled seed-coat', or in *Drosophila* a gene for each pair of bristles that is subject to genetically controlled variation. Many species have features, like individual bristles in insects, details of wing coloration in butterflies or fingerprint patterns in man, which are genetically controlled, but appear to be so trivial that they can make no difference to the survival of the individual, and can have no selective value. Such features were a problem to Darwin and to later evolutionists, because it is just these apparently useless details that are often so characteristic for each species that we use them to name or identify organisms. If these features are useless, how did they become fixed by natural selection? Genetic drift – a mechanism which could fix neutral or useless features by chance – provided a welcome explanation of such difficulties.

However, with increasing knowledge of genetics, it became evident that there is no 'gene for third pair of bristles', or 'gene for fourteenth spot on wing': these features are the end-products of an extremely complicated process (which we are still far from understanding), in which the coded information in the single nucleus of the fertilized egg is duplicated and progressively unfolded in the development of each individual. Although a pair of bristles in an insect may be inherited as if it is controlled by a single gene, it is not the direct expression of that gene: the direct product of the gene is a protein or part of a protein, and the bristles are one result of a series of interactions between this protein and hundreds or thousands of others. With this view of the genetic control of development, it became reasonable to regard bristle or fingerprint patterns, apparently non-adaptive, as outward manifestations of genes which also made other, less obvious contributions, harmful or beneficial, and so subject to selection. And for a while most biologists believed that all aspects of an organism, no matter how useless they appeared, were shaped by natural selection.

In the last few years, a new store of variation has been revealed, in the sequence of amino acids in the proteins which are the direct expression of the genes. This is studied most simply by electrophoresis, a technique which separates variant protein molecules by their response to an electric current. In section 6·1 the 169 recorded variants of human haemoglobin were mentioned, and almost every protein that is investigated is found to occur in several forms within a species. Like the deviant haemoglobins, these variants, where they have been analysed, are usually found to involve single amino acid substitutions. It becomes difficult to believe that all these variants are adaptive, and controlled by selection, and in the last few years there has been a new surge of support for random or 'non-Darwinian' evolution, regulated not by natural selection but by genetic drift – chance fluctuations in gene frequency.

This question, whether the store of genetic variation found in protein studies is controlled by selection or by random drift, is the centre of one of the great controversies in evolution theory today. The protein variants have not yet been studied for long enough to decide whether their frequency is changing in a random way or not, and it is even doubtful whether long-term studies could resolve the question. The problem is that natural selection theory says that very small selection coefficients, of the order of 1 per cent or less, are effective in causing evolutionary change, yet the demonstration of such small differences in fitness is simply not possible in experiments. It has been calculated that a 1 per cent difference in fertility between two genotypes could be shown with 95 per cent confidence only if the fertility of 130 000 females of each type were measured. If the fertility of 380 females of each type were measured, the investigator has only an even chance of detecting a much larger difference in fertility, of 10 per cent. So selection theory is trapped in its own sophistication: it asserts that small differences in fitness are effective agents of evolutionary change, yet differences of that order are not detectable in practice.

The argument between the selectionists and those who assign an important role to random effects is therefore largely confined to paper. The consequences of the two opposing theories are not sufficiently different for them to be discriminated by experiment. Mathematical tests of the random theory can be designed, but they do not give a clear-cut answer, because they are statistical tests, and the essence of the random theory is that it is an exception to the statistical norm. A further difficulty is that the two theories are not mutually exclusive. Advocates of natural selection do not assert that *all* change is guided by selection: they allow the possibility of random events in small populations. And advocates of neutral mutation and genetic drift have never supposed that these are the cause of all evolution: they agree that selection plays an important part.

I have gone into this question of random evolution in some detail, for it bears on an important philosophical point, the status of evolutionary theory as science. This point is explained more fully in chapter 12, but it can be set out briefly here. Darwinian evolution, by natural selection, predicts that organisms are as they are because all their genes have been and are being subjected to selection, those that reduce the organism's success being eliminated, and those that enhance it being favoured. This is a scientific theory, for these predictions can be tested. 'Non-Darwinian' or random evolution predicts that some features of organisms are non-adaptive, having neutral or slightly negative survival value, and that the genes controlling such features are fluctuating randomly in the population, or have been fixed because at some time in the past the population went through a bottleneck, when it was greatly reduced. When these two theories are combined, as a general explanation of evolutionary change, that general theory is no longer testable. Take natural selection: no matter how many cases fail to yield to a natural selection analysis, the theory is not threatened, for it can always be said that these failures of selection theory are explained by genetic drift. And no matter how many supposed examples of genetic drift are shown to be due, after all, to natural selection, the neutral theory is not threatened, for it never pretended to explain all evolution.

Perhaps the best we can do is to use genetic drift, as an 'explanation' of otherwise inexplicable facts, as sparingly as possible, for unless the effects of natural selection are looked for, they will not be found.

7·3   Favourable mutations

In nature, new favourable mutations must be rare. This is because existing species are the result of past selection, which will have brought them close to the best obtainable adaptation to their surroundings, so that most mutations (changes) will decrease that adaptation. As will be seen in the next section, favourable mutations are more likely in a changing or deteriorating environment, when mutations which were previously harmful may become valuable.

We have assumed that a favourable mutation appears in one member of a population. As in the case of harmful mutations, the fate of this mutant gene will be influenced by whether it is dominant, recessive, or incompletely dominant, but initially its fate is likely to be more subject to chance than is a harmful mutation. This is because beneficial mutations have a much narrower range than harmful mutations. Harmful mutations range from those with very slight effects to those which are lethal, reducing the fitness of organisms carrying them to zero. Favourable mutations with effects as drastic as lethal mutations would reduce the fitness of all other members of the species to zero: this is possible, but only in severely deteriorating environments (p. 84). In stable environments favourable mutations are likely to have small effects, and whether they increase in frequency or disappear will be much influenced by chance. The odds that a beneficial mutation will survive can be calculated, and they turn out to be very close to those for a neutral mutation. The table compares the probabilities of survival of a neutral mutation (no advantage) and a mutation conferring a 1 per cent advantage, each of which has appeared in one individual. The decimal figures may be read

Generation	No advantage	1% advantage
1	0·632	0·636
3	0·374	0·380
7	0·209	0·217
15	0·113	0·122
31	0·059	0·069
63	0·030	0·041
127	0·015	0·027

as the number of cases in a thousand in which survival is probable. Thus after fifteen generations, the favourable mutation is only likely to survive in nine more trials in a thousand than will the neutral mutation. Looked at in another way, a favourable mutation conferring a 1 per cent advantage may have to occur about fifty times before, by chance, it becomes sufficiently widespread in the population to have a secure future.

Once a favourable mutation gains a secure foothold in the population, the rate at which it will spread and replace the non-mutant alternative depends largely on whether it is dominant or recessive, just as with a harmful mutation. These two cases, a mutation giving a small advantage and one giving a small disadvantage, are two sides of the same coin, for if an advantageous mutation appears, its alternative – the existing non-mutant gene – will thereafter have a corresponding disadvantage, and the spread of the advantageous mutation will eliminate the disadvantageous, non-mutant gene. The figures mentioned in section 7·1, illustrating the slow elimination of a harmful recessive, can equally well be read as the final stages in the spread of an advantageous dominant. The different patterns of spread of a dominant or recessive favourable mutation, and elimination of a dominant or recessive harmful one are contrasted in Figure 23. The advantageous mutation, once it gains a foothold, will eventually replace its alternative, so that there will be a change in the genetic constitution of the population. This is called *directional* selection.

When considering advantageous mutations, there is one type of dominance which is particularly interesting. This is 'hybrid vigour' or 'overdominance', where both the mutant and non-mutant homozygotes are less fit than heterozygotes, with a single dose of each gene. Imagine a gene, say A_1, which codes a certain enzyme, and a partially dominant mutant form, A_2, which codes a variant protein with slightly different properties. The homozygotes, having constitutions A_1A_1 or A_2A_2, will each have only one form of enzyme, but the heterozygotes, A_1A_2, will have both, and might function more efficiently because of this. In such cases, although natural selection will tend to eliminate both types of homozygous individuals, selection will not result in the elimination of either gene, but in a polymorphic population, with the two genes present in proportions which are governed by the relative disadvantage of each homozygote to the heterozygote. Even if one of the homozygous conditions is lethal, selection will preserve that gene. Suppose that A_2 is lethal in homozygotes (A_2A_2 has fitness zero) and A_1 homozygotes suffer a 5 per cent disadvantage relative to the heterozygote (i.e. A_1A_1 has fitness 0.95; A_1A_2 has fitness one). After many generations, the result of this situation will be a stable population containing two or three lethal homozygotes per thousand individuals, about ninety per thousand heterozygotes, and the rest A_1A_1 homozygotes. If the two homozygotes are equally fit, the result of selection will be a population containing 25 per cent of each homozygote and 50 per cent heterozygotes. Where there are three (or more) alternative forms of the gene the situation is more complicated, but selection will again produce a polymorphic population. This sort of selection, due to hybrid vigour and resulting in stable polymorphism, is called *balancing* selection. It is a type of selection that will preserve variation within a population.

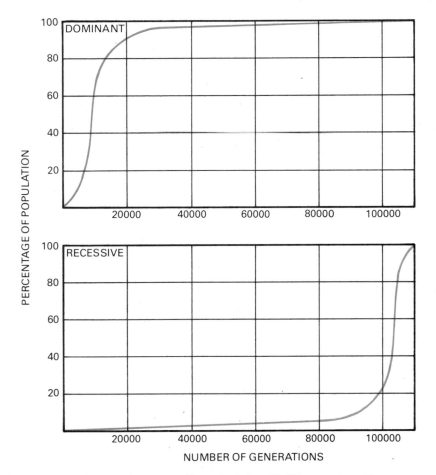

Figure 23

The spread of dominant and recessive mutations. The graphs contrast the spread of a mutation giving an advantage of one in a thousand (fitness = 1·001) when it is dominant (above) or recessive. The dominant mutation spreads through 90 per cent of the population quite rapidly, but is still not fixed after 100 000 generations. The recessive mutation spreads very slowly until it is present in about 10 per cent of the population, and then becomes fixed quite quickly. These are ideal curves, showing the calculated rate of increase and neglecting chance fluctuations.

This account of selection theory – considering the fate of various types of point mutation – has been long and probably heavy going. The theory is, in fact, even more complicated. In this chapter, I have discussed selection of a point mutation as if each gene could be considered in isolation, but it cannot. Genes do not exist in isolation, but in chromosomes, and although chromosomes are mixed up with their homologues by crossing-over, and can be broken up by chromosome mutations such as translocations, there is still strong linkage between adjacent genes on the chromosome. So the prospects of a gene may be influenced by its neighbours – a neutral mutation might spread through the population by selection because it lies next to, and so is linked with, another gene that is subject to strong selection. Natural selection theory also has to account for the spread of chromosome mutations – inversions, translocations, etc. (section 6·2). For example, the six inversions which distinguish human and chimpanzee chromosomes must each have originated in one individual in the ancestry of one species or the other, and spread through the population in the same way as a point mutation. Natural selection theory has to consider chromosomes and pieces of chromosome, as well as individual genes.

It will be as well to summarize selection theory as briefly as possible. Mutations are random events, the result of accidental errors in replication of DNA or in nuclear division. A mutant DNA molecule or chromosome has no chance of propagating itself unless it arises in a sex cell or in a cell which will produce sex cells. Its fate will then depend on three factors: on chance; on whether a mutant gene is dominant, recessive or intermediate; and on whether its effects are harmful, beneficial or neutral. A mutation can only be categorized as harmful or beneficial after observing the performance of its carriers. The effects of a mutation can never be shown to be completely neutral.

The terms 'harmful' and 'favourable' or 'beneficial' refer to reproductive success, and can be graded on a scale of fitness. This term is relative, because we can only compare the fitness of one genotype with another, and in a particular environment. In nature, the great majority of mutations will be harmful, since existing species, because of past selection, should already be closely adapted to their environments.

Chance is most important in the early stages of the career of a mutation, when it is present in only one or a few individuals, but chance may also play a large part in small populations. On average, a harmful mutation will eventually be eliminated, by poor reproductive performance of individuals carrying it, and the species will be preserved unchanged by stabilizing selection. On average, an advantageous mutation will eventually become widespread, by poor reproductive performance of individuals carrying the original, non-mutant gene, and the constitution of the species will change, by directional selection. Balancing selection is the case when heterozygotes are fitter than either mutant or non-mutant homozygotes – it results in polymorphism or the preservation of variation. Genetic drift, the chance fixation of neutral or harmful mutations in small populations, should be invoked as sparingly as possible.

8 Selection in action

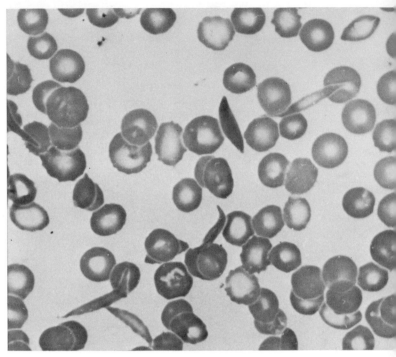

Figure 24
Sickle-cell blood.
A photomicrograph
of a blood-smear
from a person
heterozygous for the
sickle-cell gene.
Amongst the normal
rounded cells, there
are a few elongated
cells, distorted by
crystallization of the
abnormal
haemoglobin.
Enlarged about 1200
times.

This chapter will examine five examples of natural selection that have been observed and analysed during the last fifty years. They illustrate various aspects of selection theory described in the last chapter.

8·1 Sickle-cell anaemia

In section 6·1, on mutation, the many known variants of human haemoglobin were mentioned. Some of these cause no obvious ill-effects in their carriers, but one, known as haemoglobin-S, produces a severe disability, sickle-cell anaemia. This disease is so called because some of the red blood cells of afflicted people are not disc-shaped, as in normal blood, but sickle- or spindle-shaped (Fig. 24). Analysis of these red cells shows that the only difference from normal red cells is a single amino acid substitution in the beta chain of the haemoglobin – valine instead of glutamine at position six. It is therefore caused by a point mutation in DNA, substitution of 'T' for 'A' in the middle of the triplet, and is due to a single mutant gene which we can symbolize as Hs, with Hn for the normal gene.

Sickle-cell anaemia is a severe disability, and usually causes death before adolescence. Studies of its inheritance show that this severe, fatal anaemia is manifested only in homozygous individuals, who have received the mutant gene from both parents and have the genotype HsHs. In heterozygotes (HnHs), who have received the mutant gene from only one parent, the red blood cells may show slight distortion when the oxygen concentration in the blood is very low, but these people are not anaemic and can lead normal lives.

Sickle-cell anaemia is found in three main areas, central Africa, in a zone extending through the eastern Mediterranean, Middle East and India to the Far East (Fig. 25), and in North and Central America. The key to this distribution was found in Africa, where the proportion of heterozygotes for the sickle gene is as high as 40 per cent in some districts. These districts are found to be those where the most severe form of malaria, malignant tertian or falciparum, is prevalent. Malaria is caused by minute, single-celled parasites, which are introduced into the blood by the bite of a mosquito, and then undergo growth and asexual reproduction cycles actually inside red blood cells, where they feed by breaking down haemoglobin. People with normal haemoglobin (genotype HnHn) are susceptible to this severe, and often fatal disease. But those who are heterozygous for the sickle-cell trait (genotype HnHs) are much more resistant to malaria because infected cells tend to 'sickle' or collapse, interfering with the development of the parasite. So in areas where falciparum malaria is prevalent, sickle-cell heterozygotes are fitter than either the sickle-cell homozygote, who dies in childhood of anaemia, or the normal homozygote, who may die of malaria, also usually in childhood. The high proportion of sickle-cell heterozygotes in parts of Africa is therefore caused by balancing selection, where a mutant gene which is lethal in homozygotes is preserved by selection because of the increased fitness of heterozygotes in the malarial environment.

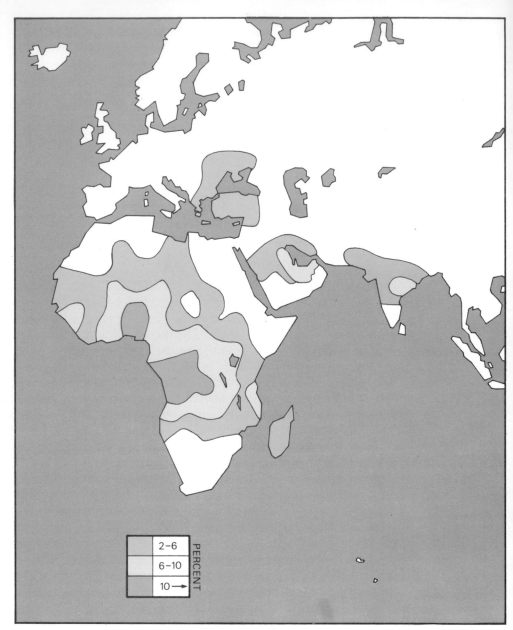

Figure 25
The distribution of the sickle-cell gene in the
human population of the Old World. The highest
incidence is in West Africa, which was the source
of most of the slaves transported to the New
World.

The slave trade gave a new twist to the sickle-cell story. This forced emigration introduced large numbers of Africans carrying the sickle-cell gene into America. Through subsequent migrations, the gene is now widespread in North and South America, and also occurs in Britain. In Central America there are malarial districts where the gene is present in up to 20 per cent of the population, but in North America there is little or no falciparum malaria, so the selective agent which was maintaining the polymorphism is no longer active. The average incidence of the sickle-cell gene in North American negroes is less than 5 per cent. In the absence of malaria, the sickle-cell gene is effectively recessive, heterozygotes having no obvious advantage or disadvantage over normal homozygotes. So in North America at present there is a situation like that outlined on p. 65, where a lethal recessive is widespread, and where heterozygotes can be identified (by blood tests). These heterozygotes will be advised not to marry another carrier of the gene, but as was shown on p. 65, that will not reduce the frequency of the gene. Should these people be advised not to reproduce at all, to avoid propagating the gene? Not in a free society.

Sickle-cell anaemia illustrates several points: the possible lethal effects of a single point mutation; balancing selection, leading to a stable polymorphism; the fact that fitness is determined by the environment, the superior fitness of heterozygotes depending on whether they are in malarial areas or not; and the difficult ethical decisions involved in genetic counselling.

8·2 Industrial melanism

This phenomenon (industrial blackening) has appeared in many insects during the last 150 years, as one consequence of the industrial revolution. In the neighbourhood of industrial towns and cities, the buildings, rocks and tree trunks become blackened by deposits of soot, and the lichens and other simple plants that usually colonize such surfaces are killed. These changes have evoked a rapid and obvious evolutionary response in the British peppered moth, *Biston betularia*. This, like most moths, is nocturnal, flying by night and resting by day on surfaces such as tree trunks. The typical form of the moth has pale wings with small black markings, and

Figure 26
The peppered moth, *Biston betularia*.
On the left is a tree trunk encrusted with lichens,
from an unpolluted rural area, and on the right a
soot-covered tree from an industrial city. On each
there is one melanic moth and one pale, typical
form.

on lichen-covered tree trunks it is almost invisible. In all eighteenth- and early nineteenth-century insect collections, the moth has this coloration. In 1849 a single melanic or black example was caught, near Manchester, and by 1900, 98 or 99 per cent of moths collected near Manchester were black. In the 1870s black individuals were still quite uncommon, but in the 1880s they already outnumbered the pale form. In the Manchester district, this change from a pale-coloured population of the peppered moth to a 98 per cent dark population took about fifty years, and this period corresponds with the most rapid increase in the human population of Manchester, and in the quantity of coal burned there. The same change occurred around other industrial cities, and also in some nearby rural, unpolluted areas.

The differences between the pale peppered moth (form *typica*) and the dark variety (*carbonaria*) is due to a single dominant mutation, so that homozygotes and heterozygotes for the mutation are both black. There is also another, less common dark form (*insularia*) which is produced by another mutation of the same gene, dominant to *typica* but recessive to *carbonaria*. The selective agent which caused the rapid spread of the dark form in industrial areas, and the virtual elimination of the pale form, is predation by birds. The melanic mutations have presumably been turning up spontaneously for hundreds of years, but the mutant moths would be very conspicuous in the usual resting places of the species – lichen-covered tree trunks – and would be seen and eaten by birds. With the advent of industrial pollution, the mutant form was suddenly at an advantage, for it is nearly invisible on blackened tree trunks, where the pale *typica* is highly conspicuous (Fig. 26).

That birds do selectively eat those moths which contrast with their background has been demonstrated by experiments in which large numbers of moths are marked (with a spot of paint on the underside), and some are then released and observed in a polluted wood, and others in an unpolluted wood. After a day or two, light traps are set at night, and the number of marked moths trapped is recorded. Observations showed that birds were taking the conspicuous moths on tree trunks, and trapping showed that the proportion of pale moths was significantly reduced in the polluted wood, and that fewer dark moths were recaptured in the unpolluted wood. The intensity of selection against the pale moths around Manchester in the second half of the nineteenth century can be estimated, and works out at between 30 and 50 per cent. This is extraordinarily high, but similar intense selection pressure was found in the releasing and trapping experiments. During the last fifteen or twenty years, smoke-control policies have been introduced in industrial cities, and the peppered moth has already begun to respond: in some places the proportion of pale forms has increased by about 5 per cent since 1960.

The spread of melanic forms in the peppered moth is not an isolated instance. More than a hundred insect species show similar changes in Britain, and there are many other examples in Europe and North America. The mechanism of these changes is not always the same. In some species the darkening is controlled by several genes; in others the dominance of the dark mutation is incomplete, so that the heterozygotes are intermediate in colour; and a couple of cases are known where the dark mutant is recessive, and is increasing relatively slowly. In peppered moths, and in some other species, there is evidence that the homozygous mutant forms are less fit than the hetero-

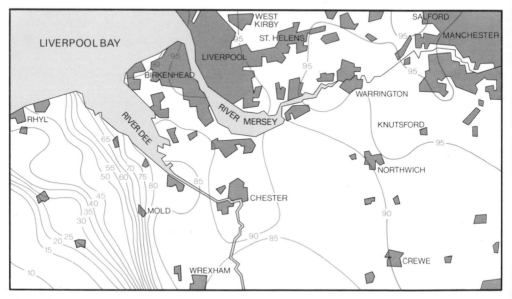

Figure 27
The distribution of light and dark forms of the peppered moth around Liverpool, England, in the early 1970s. The contours show the percentage of dark forms in the moth population: they are very common in the urban and industrial areas to the north and east, but their numbers fall away rapidly towards the south-west, in rural Wales.

zygotes, suffering some disadvantage, perhaps physiological. This situation would lead to a balanced polymorphism, as in sickle-cell anaemia, and several insect species maintain a polymorphic population of light and dark forms in unpolluted countryside, providing a ready source of variation if pollution increases. There is also some evidence in the peppered moth that the intensity of coloration in the dark variety has increased during this century, and that the advantage of heterozygotes has also increased during this period. Both these changes could be explained by selection favouring modifying genes which enhance the effects of the melanic mutation.

Industrial melanism brings out several aspects of natural selection. Perhaps the most important is the demonstration that directional selection, leading to a change in the gene-pool of a species, is caused by changes in the environment. It is also obvious that the fitness of any mutation is determined by the environment – the black mutation is harmful in smoke-free areas, advantageous in industrial areas. The intensity of selection pressures in the spread of melanism, 30–50 per cent, is also striking – a single point mutation may give greatly increased fitness, and may initiate very rapid change. The increase in pale moths since the introduction of smoke-control shows how rapid and sensitive selection may be. Finally, there is the suggestion that modifying genes have been selected which enhance the effects of the black mutation – this illustrates the point that an organism is not the result of a series of genes acting independently. The action of a single gene is subject to control by and interaction with other genes, so that selective change will involve an integrated set of genes.

8·3   Resistance to antibiotics

Antibiotics are substances, naturally produced by some micro-organisms, which inhibit the growth of other micro-organisms when present in extremely small quantities. The best known antibiotic, penicillin, is produced by a mould, *Penicillium chrysogenum*, and is active against a wide range of disease-producing bacteria. Penicillin was discovered in 1928, and was isolated and produced commercially during the Second World War. Since then, more than a thousand similar substances have been found, and many have come into commercial production – actinomycin, aureomycin, neomycin, streptomycin, tetracyclines and other familiar names. This variety is not simply due to competition between drug companies – it is a response to evolution of resistance, by natural selection, in disease-producing bacteria.

Under favourable conditions, bacteria may divide (reproduce) every twenty or thirty minutes and, because of their very small size, a person suffering from a bacterial infection may harbour a population of bacteria many times as great as the human population of the world. If treated with an antibiotic, such a person may make a rapid recovery, but to the bacteria the antibiotic appears as a catastrophic change in a previously benign environment. For example, penicillin acts by preventing the formation of bacterial cell wall, so stopping cell division. Other antibiotics inhibit protein synthesis, or damage the surface membrane of the bacteria. But in such enormous populations, the possibility of a spontaneous mutation giving resistance to the antibiotic may be very high. The human colon bacillus, *Escherichia coli*, has a resistance mutation rate to streptomycin of between one in a hundred million and one in a thousand million cell divisions. Since a single bacterium may produce ten thousand million descendants within twenty-four hours, these odds become quite low, and resistance to streptomycin and other antibiotics is a common occurrence. Some of these resistant strains turn out to be streptomycin dependent, and cannot live without the antibiotic, but back mutations to the original constitution occur at about the same rate, so that a two-mutation process – extraordinarily unlikely in one individual, but quite probable in a population numbered in billions – will enable a bacterial strain to survive streptomycin treatment unchanged.

Antibiotic-resistant bacteria show the maximum possible rate of evolution by natural selection – all other members of the population are unable to grow, and have fitness zero, while the resistant mutant has fitness one, and replaces the non-resistant form almost instantaneously.

Before leaving bacteria and antibiotics, it is worth mentioning commercial production of penicillin as an example of extremely successful artificial selection. The original strain of *Penicillium chrysogenum* had a yield of penicillin that we can call 1·0. A spontaneous mutation selected from the cultures increased this yield to 2·5. Cultures subjected to X-rays produced a mutant with a yield of 5, and then exposure of this form to ultraviolet light induced a further mutation, yielding 9. Subsequent treatment with ultraviolet light and mustard gas threw up successive mutant strains with yields 20, 25, 30, and eventually 50 times as much as the original strain.

The development of antibiotic-resistant strains of bacteria, and also of insects resistant to DDT and a host of other recently discovered insecticides, are genuine evolutionary changes. By indiscriminately spraying insecticides and prescribing antibiotics we change the environment, and natural selection ensures that where a species throws up an advantageous mutation, it is propagated and the genetic constitution of the species changes.

8·4   Shell pattern in snails

Cepaea nemoralis is a common snail in Britain and Europe, widespread in woods, fields, hedgerows, scrubland, sand dunes and so on. The shells of this species are extraordinarily diverse: the ground colour may be various shades of brown,

Figure 28
The snail *Cepaea nemoralis*.
These shells were collected from a single population · in Cornwall, England. The bands are counted on the largest whorl of the shell. Upper row, left to right, unbanded, one-banded and two-banded.

Lower row, left to right, three-banded, four-banded, five-banded, and a form in which the upper and lower groups of bands are widened so that they run together, producing two very broad bands. The scale is in millimetres.

yellow or pink, and the shell may be plain or girdled by dark brown bands, one to five in number and varying in width (Fig. 28). One population of snails will include a number of these variants, and a neighbouring population may have a different set of patterns. These shell patterns are inherited, and are controlled by a complex of genes. The ground colour of the shell is determined by one gene with at least six, and possibly as many as eight, alternative forms (alleles). Brown is dominant to three different pink alleles, and these are dominant to two different yellows. In shell banding, 'no bands' is dominant to 'banded'; at least two other genes control the number of bands; and another gene controls the width of the bands.

Since the environments occupied by snail colonies with different shell patterns seemed to be much the same, it was at first assumed that the variations were random and due to genetic drift. But more detailed investigation has shown that much of this variation is due to selection, and that the situation is also more complicated than was originally supposed.

As in the peppered moth, birds are the selective agent responsible for some of the shell variation. Thrushes are fond of snails, and in order to eat them they pick up a snail, carry it a short distance to a suitable stone, and then drop or tap the snail on the stone until the shell shatters. The broken shells around these thrush 'anvils' provide a record of the snails actually collected and eaten by birds, and the proportion of each variant can be compared with those represented in the surviving population. Comparisons of this sort, in a variety of habitats and at different times of year, show that thrushes pick out snails that contrast with the background, so that in woods with little undergrowth or on open downland banded shells are at a disadvantage, while in woods with undergrowth and in scrub unbanded shells will be selected out. The ground colour is also selected to match the habitat. But there is also a seasonal effect: in winter and early spring, brown and pink shells are favoured, while in late spring and summer, when the background is greener, yellow shells are favoured. In this way, a polymorphic population may be maintained in one place because selection favours different forms at different seasons, or at different stages in the life cycle.

Bird predation is not the only factor influencing the snail polymorphism. Some shell-colour genes also have physiological effects, since some variants have advantages in warm conditions and others in cold. Local variation within populations is influenced by microclimatic factors such as the accumulation of cold air in small hollows. Yet another complicating factor is that birds may learn to recognize, and search for, the snail shell pattern that is most abundant; rare patterns may escape notice not because they are inconspicuous but because the bird does not recognize them as its usual food. This sort of *frequency-dependent selection* will favour the rarer variants, but as they become more abundant their advantage will fall off.

There is also a large-scale polymorphism in *Cepaea nemoralis*, where many colonies over a large area show a certain uniformity, and are separated from neighbouring population groups by quite sharp boundaries, where a different variation pattern takes over. The mechanism behind this is not understood.

We are still far from understanding or explaining all the variation in *Cepaea* shells, within and between populations. But the complexity of the interacting factors (predation, seasonal variation, multiple genetic control, physiological differences, frequency effects) makes *Cepaea* a more realistic example of natural selection than the simpler situations like sickle-cell anaemia and industrial melanism.

8·5   Social insects

Insects which live in highly organized societies – termites, bees, wasps and ants – have always fascinated naturalists. Darwin was the first to explain how the remarkable instincts which govern insect societies could be produced by natural selection, and very recently the sex ratio in social insects has been used as a test of a modern variant of selection theory – *kin selection*.

In the social Hymenoptera (the group of four-winged insects that includes ants, bees and wasps), each colony or nest contains one or more fertile females (the queens), a number of fertile males (the drones or kings), and many sterile females (the workers). In ants, the workers are often of several different kinds or castes, such as soldiers, indoor workers and outdoor workers, and these worker castes may differ in size and structure, as well as in behaviour. The organization of insect societies may be very complicated, with strange echoes of traits of human societies. For example, some ants are stock-farmers, keeping aphids which they 'milk' for honeydew, care for in the nest, and carry out to the food plants; other ants are gardeners, cultivating yeasts or fungi in the nest. In some ant species the workers are incapable of caring for the nest, or even of feeding themselves, but spend their working hours raiding the nests of other species, and capturing the larvae or pupae, which they carry back to their own nest. When these captives hatch, they behave as they would have done at home, caring for their captors and the captors' young, as slaves. In *The Origin of Species* Darwin wrote a fine account of these slave-making ants, and his observations of them. They attracted his interest because this system, in which animals of one species devote themselves to the welfare of another, seems inexplicable by natural selection, for selection can only promote the successful, and to live in slavery is no success.

Darwin was able to show that the dependence of slave-making ants on their slaves is less in one species than in another, and less in one geographic race of a single species than in another. He guessed that slave-making originated in the habit of carrying home, as food, larvae and pupae of other species: some of these might hatch and work, instinctively, as slaves, and natural selection would favour the slave-makers devoting themselves to the collection of pupae not as food but as potential slaves. The slaves themselves will be incapable of any long-term retaliation through natural selection, for they are sterile workers, and cannot pass on their genes.

Yet the origin of these sterile worker castes in social insects poses another puzzle for natural selection: why should it favour the loss of reproductive potential in most individuals of a species? Darwin wrote of these sterile workers as a 'special difficulty, which at first appeared to me insuperable, and actually fatal to my whole theory'. The main difficulty he had in mind was not the sterility of the worker caste (we now know that this is usually the result of environmental factors, especially the food given to the larva), but the difference in form between the workers and their parents, and between the different castes of workers. For the structure of the workers could never be directly affected by natural selection, since they produce no offspring. Darwin's explanation included an analogy with the division of labour in human society, and the comment 'selection has been applied to the family, not the individual'. These ideas have been taken much further in the modern theory of kin selection.

In many ant species all the members of a colony share the same mother and father – the inseminated queen who founded the colony. Thus the colony is a family, consisting of brothers and sisters. This fact is the key to the altruistic behaviour of the workers, sterile females who devote themselves to the care of their mother and her offspring, their brothers and sisters. The colony can be thought of as one organism, in which the division of labour amongst the worker castes is analogous to the division of labour between different cell types or organs in an individual animal. Our blood cells and liver cells, for example, have lost the possibility of contributing to the next generation, except vicariously, through the egg or sperm cells that they may help to nourish. In the same way, the worker ants cannot reproduce themselves, but they can help to contribute to the next generation by caring for the queen and her eggs and young, their brothers and sisters. The slave workers in the nests of slave-making ants are deceived, by their instincts, into caring for the young of another species: their altruism is misdirected. We can ask how close should the relationship be, between the altruist and the recipient of her kindness, for self-sacrifice to be worthwhile. The theory of kin selection answers this question.

In sexual species like our own, each individual receives half of his or her genes from one parent, and half from the other. Our genetic relationship to each of our parents, and to each of our children, is therefore one-half. Our parents, in turn, each received half of their genes from one of our four grandparents, so that our genetic relationship to each grandparent, and to each grandchild, is one-quarter. For brothers and sisters (excluding identical twins, where the relationship is one), the argument is a little more complicated, because of the way in which the parental genes and chromosomes are shuffled in the production of eggs and sperm (section 5·4). Genetic relationship between brother and sister ranges from almost nil (in the very unlikely case when the two happen to get opposite halves of both the maternal and paternal sets of genes) to almost one (when they receive the same half of both sets of genes, equally unlikely), but on average it is one-half, the same as the parent/child relationship. Your aunts and uncles, or nephews and nieces, share, on average, one-quarter of your genes; the first-cousin relationship is one-eighth, the half-brother one-quarter, and so on.

Given these degrees of relationship, we can frame a theory of the evolution of altruism by natural selection. It is worth laying down your life to save three of your children, or three of your brothers and sisters, because their combined genes represent one-and-a-half of yours. It is not worth laying down your life for five cousins ($\frac{5}{8}$) or three grandchildren ($\frac{3}{4}$), although in the latter case you might reflect that if your reproductive life was finished, and theirs just beginning, the unselfish act would be to your genetic advantage. Is there anything more to this theory than a morbid parlour-game, or the basis for heartless jokes about mothers-in-law (relationship nil)? So far, only one situation has been found where the theory has consequences which can be tested, by confrontation with nature. This test of kin selection is also a unique example of a mathematical test of natural selection which is made in nature, and not on paper or in a laboratory experiment.

The test involves the social insects, and hinges on their peculiar method of sex determination. In Hymenoptera (ants, bees, wasps, etc.) fertilized eggs develop into females, and unfertilized eggs into males. This system is also found in some mites, and in a few other insects. Why it developed is not known. It is called *haplo-diploidy*, for it means that females are diploid formed by the fusion of two gametes, each carrying a haploid set of genes, and males are haploid, having only the genes from one gamete. Because of this, the genetic relationships in ants, bees and wasps are peculiar. Males, developed from unfertilized eggs, have received all their genes from the mother, and have a genetic relationship with her of one, not one-half as in other sexual organisms. Females receive half their genes from the mother and half from the father, and so have the usual one-half relationship with each parent, but since the father has only a haploid set of genes, all his sperm are identical, and sisters are therefore related not by one-half, as is usual but by three-quarters (an average of one-quarter, through the mother, as usual, added to one-half, through the identical paternal contribution). The brother/sister relationship is not the normal one-half, but a quarter: the brother has only half as many genes as his sister, and has received them all from the mother. They may be the same half as his sister has (relationship $\frac{1}{2}$, very unlikely) or the opposite half (relationship nil, equally unlikely), and the relationship averages out at a quarter.

In an ant nest, therefore, the workers are caring for their mother (relationship $\frac{1}{2}$) and her offspring, their brothers (relationship $\frac{1}{4}$) and sisters (relationship $\frac{3}{4}$). In working to bring up sisters (relationship $\frac{3}{4}$), a worker can contribute more to the next generation than by investing an equal amount of energy in bringing up her own daughters (relationship $\frac{1}{2}$). Hence the tendency for sterile female castes to develop in haplo-diploid insects. The theory also says that workers should devote three times as much energy to raising fertile sisters (potential queens) as they should to raising males, because they share three-quarters of their genes with sisters, and only a quarter with their brothers. This prediction of the theory can be tested. A rough estimate of the energy invested by workers in raising fertile males and females is the weight of individuals of each sex produced, since the weight represents the result of feeding by the workers. Workers at Harvard University, who published the results of the test in 1976, obtained estimates of the sex ratio in nests of 21 species of ants, and corrected them by a factor allowing for the differences in weight between males and females in each species. The resulting figure, or 'investment ratio', was $1:3\cdot45$ averaged over all the species, compared with the prediction from theory of $1:3$.

These figures are close to the predicted ratio, but a most interesting control test is possible, by comparing this ratio with that in slave-making ants, where, as outlined above, the workers are raising the offspring of another species, and so should have no interest in their sex ratio. In slave-making species, the sex ratio should instead be controlled by the queen, who would benefit most from a $1:1$ ratio, since her relationship to both sons and daughters is one-half. The 'investment ratio' has been estimated in nests of two species of slave-making ant, and found to be $1:1$ on average. Even more remarkable is that one of these slave-making species enslaves workers of a species which produce a $1:3$ ratio of investment when working for their own queen. These results are consistent with the theory of kin selection, and with no other theory yet conceived. How they are to be explained in detail is not yet known. For example, how can it be that potential slave ants 'know' that when they are in their own nest, a $1:3$ ratio of investment is to their advantage, and how can they be 'told', when enslaved, that their new queen 'wants' a $1:1$ ratio? We can be sure that the words 'know', 'told' and 'wants' here are short-hand for some other expression, perhaps of the form 'natural selection has adjusted the genes governing behaviour, or governing the hormonal or nutritional regime of the workers' In any case, the social insects, far from being a 'special diffi culty' (Darwin's words) for natural selection, are proving to be a goldmine for the theory, especially for the theory of kin selection. This theory, successfully applied to genetically con trolled behaviour in insects, is by no means uncontroversial when applied to other animals. Its application to mankind is mentioned in section 14.2.

9 The origin of species

We now come back to the problem posed in the title of Darwin's book – can the genetic and environmental factors discussed in the last four chapters account for the division of one species into two, or the appearance of new species? There is one genetic mechanism that produces new species instantly – polyploidy or chromosome-doubling (section 6·3). This is important in plants, but not in animals, where we have to find other reasons for species formation.

9·1 Inconstant environments

Natural selection acts on heritable variations produced by the different types of mutation. But mutation only provides the raw material for selection; a new mutation will not increase in frequency and displace the non-mutant gene unless it is favoured by the environment, and this is most likely in a changed or changing environment. This idea, of an inconstant environment, is the key to species formation. It is commonplace that environmental conditions vary with distance, on a large scale – a holiday in the Canaries will be more enjoyable than one in Spitsbergen – and on a small scale – the daffodils come out earlier in one corner of the garden than in another. We also know that environmental conditions in one place vary with time – Britain was under the Arctic ice sheet in geologically recent times, and most of it was under the ocean not long before that. The relatively new information on continental drift (see Fig. 38) shows that the concept 'in one place' does not maintain its everyday meaning over long periods of time – India was once joined to Antarctica and the other southern continents and was under ice, while Antarctica itself was once in the temperate zone.

Knowledge of genetics compels us to think of species not as collections of similar individuals, but as collections of genes or *gene-pools*. These are more or less completely isolated from the gene-pools of other species, persist through time, and are reshuffled in each generation by the chances of mating to produce new mixtures, which are expressed in the phenotypes of individuals. The fact that each individual requires a certain amount of space makes it unlikely that all individuals of a species will be exposed to exactly the same environment. And the larger the population of a species, the more space it must occupy, and the more likely it is that environmental changes will be encountered. Within each species, new mutations are constantly appearing, and the larger the population, the more mutations will appear.

In nature, no species occupies every part of the region through which it occurs. *Homo sapiens*, the most widespread species (except for certain human parasites), is not evenly distributed over the land masses of the world. There are large areas – the Arctic, Antarctic, major deserts and mountain ranges – which are virtually without human population, and within populated regions people are not equally spread, but aggregated into settlements, of varying size, which are separated by thinly populated or uninhabited areas. Species of plants and animals are distributed in just the same way. The original reason for the location of a human settlement can often be found. It may be availability of fresh water, or of level ground suitable for planting, or of a site offering protection from attack. The reasons for the patchy distribution of other species may be harder to guess, but similar factors are involved. Perhaps a local variation in soil allows a particular plant species to establish a colony; insects which feed on that plant will follow, and then species which prey on the insects will arrive. Even the open ocean, which appears to us as a uniform mass of water, is broken up into different habitats by currents, temperature variations, areas of upwelling or sinking water, and so on.

9·2   Barriers to gene exchange

In the human species, each individual may, in theory, choose as a mate any individual (of the opposite sex and of appropriate age) from the whole population of the globe. But in practice, we know that it does not work out like this. Even today, when international travel and social mobility are relatively easy, an individual is most likely to marry a close neighbour, if not the girl or boy next door (Fig. 29). Oceans, or national frontiers, will act as barriers, reducing the probabilities of matings across them. In other species, the choice of mate is limited by similar factors – distance and natural barriers between colonies.

Every species is thus broken up into more or less separate, inbreeding populations. Chance migrations, temporary expansions of colonies and other fluctuations make it unlikely that such populations will be completely isolated from each other. In genetic terms, a species will be split up into a number of partially distinct gene-pools, with restricted gene exchange (or *gene flow*) between them. Each of these populations will be exposed to slightly different environmental conditions, and over long periods of time natural selection may fix different mutations in different populations. If interbreeding or gene exchange between neighbouring populations is fairly frequent, such local genetic differentiation may not proceed far, but in a widespread species gene exchange between populations at opposite ends of the range will be virtually nil. These terminal populations will never interbreed directly, and will only be able to exchange genes by means of gene flow through interbreeding between the chain of populations linking the ends of the range. There is an analogy in dogs, where interbreeding between a great dane and a chihuahua is not possible because of gross disparity in size, but great danes and chihuahuas could exchange genes at one or more removes, because they are linked by a series of intermediate breeds which can mate with one another.

In nature, widely-separated populations of a species may be exposed to very different environments, and may, in consequence, accumulate many genetic differences. The contrast between an Australian aborigine and an Eskimo is an obvious example of this, as are ring-species, like the herring and lesser black-backed gulls described in section 3·2. The accumulated genetic changes differentiating Australian aborigines and Eskimos do not, so far as we know, impair fertility between the two races in any way. In Britain, the herring gull and lesser black-backed gull are the two terminal populations of a circumpolar ring-species. They are interfertile, but breeding between them is so rare that there is virtually no gene exchange. The reason that these two populations remain separate is behavioural. Neighbouring colonies of the two species nest in slightly different habitats, and mate selection, by the female gull, depends on recognition of males as

95

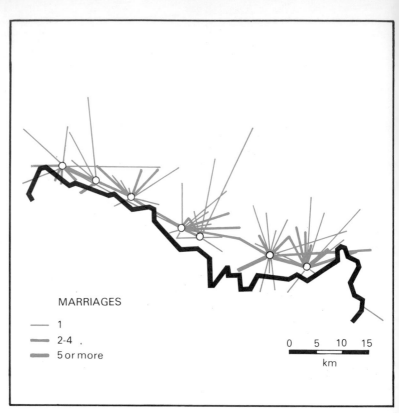

MARRIAGES

— 1
— 2-4 .
— 5 or more

0　5　10　15
km

members of her own species, particularly by the colour of the ring surrounding the eye. Experiments in which eggs of one species are transferred into nests of the other show that this recognition symbol is learnt, by the mechanism known as imprinting. Newly-hatched chicks will recognize as their mother the first creature they see, and in adult life will expect their mates to show the same visual signals.

Unlike the mechanisms described in section 5·1, the barrier separating herring and lesser black-backed gulls is behavioural, rather than purely genetic. But the ability to 'imprint' the mother is inborn in chicks, and so must also be genetic. However, there is one non-genetic barrier that will prevent hybridization between two populations: *geographic isolation.* The gene-pools of Australian aborigines and Eskimos were, until the last couple of hundred years, isolated from one another almost as effectively as those of a fish and an insect. But if two or more species are to co-exist in the same place, some more positive mechanism must prevent hybridization. Behavioural differences, like those between the two species of

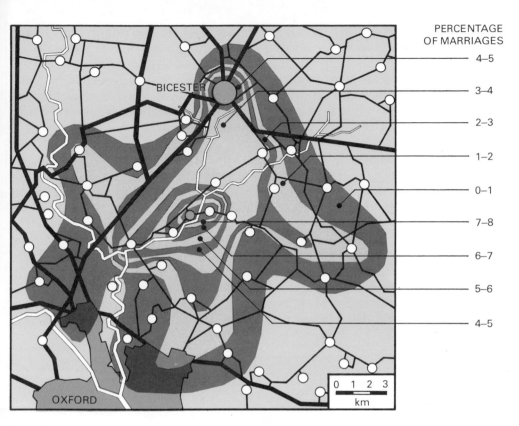

Figure 29

Barriers to gene exchange.
Diagrams showing how human populations tend to maintain their genetic isolation, by choice of marriage partners from the immediate neighbourhood. Opposite, a political boundary as a barrier to marriage. The circles are villages on the German side of the pre-war frontier between Germany and Moravia (black line). The coloured lines show the direction, distance and number of marriages made by the villagers.

Above, the grey contours show the source of marriage partners for the villagers of Charlton on Otmoor, England (the green circle in the centre of the map) over a 360-year period. The choice of marriage partners is not governed by distance alone. Apart from the concentration on the market town of Bicester, the contours show a trend following the road (black) and river (white) to the south-west of Charlton, whereas the Otmoor, the roadless area south of the village, has acted as a barrier. The river Cherwell, running near the left-hand edge of the map, has also been a barrier, although it is only a couple of metres wide.

gull, can operate only in animals with internal fertilization or fairly elaborate pairing behaviour (such recognition signals need not be visual – difference in song in birds, frogs and grasshoppers may be as effective). In plants, and in animals with simpler courtship, other genetically-controlled mechanisms come into play. In addition to those mentioned in section 5·1 – lack of attraction between gametes, hybrid inviability, hybrid sterility – the two most widespread mechanisms are *ecological* or *habitat isolation*, and *seasonal isolation*.

Habitat isolation is a situation where two populations live in the same region, but in slightly different habitats – two plant populations might live at different altitudes or on different soil types; two insect populations might feed and breed in the same place, but on different species of plant; two fish populations may live in water of different temperature or salinity. Many examples of this sort are to be found.

Seasonal isolation is the situation where two populations do not interbreed because they mate at different times. The classic example is in cicadas, a group of insects with a very long underground larval stage in the life cycle (Fig. 30). In North America there are two species-groups of cicadas, one completing the life cycle in thirteen years, the other in seventeen years. In any one locality, a brood of cicadas will only emerge once every thirteen or seventeen years (except in the few places where both types occur together), but the broods of each type are not synchronized over large areas, so that in the range of 13-year cicadas a brood will emerge in one place in one year, and in

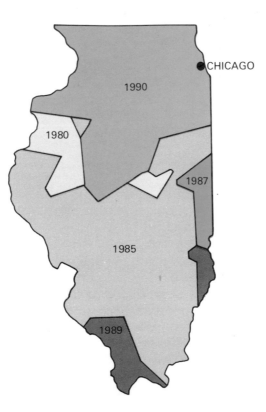

Figure 30
The distribution of cicada broods in Illinois.
The grey areas are those of 13-year cicadas, and the green those of 17-year cicadas. The dates indicate the next year of emergence of each brood. The numbers thirteen and seventeen were probably not selected at random: both are prime numbers, not divisible by any smaller number, so that any predator with a shorter life cycle cannot adjust it to coincide with the cicadas at every second or third generation.

a nearby place the next year. Gene exchange between these broods is prevented as effectively as if they lived thousands of kilometres apart. Many less spectacular examples of seasonal isolation are known.

9·3 Genetic differences between species, populations and individuals

Failure in hybridization between different species, in nature or in experiments, is an indication that they are reproductively isolated. It can also be looked at in another way – as one of the ways of estimating the genetic difference between two similar species. Such estimates are most easily made when hybrids can be obtained, especially second generation hybrids, in which the genes of the two species will combine to throw up many variants. These variations are an indication of the number of genetic differences between the two species. This technique is sometimes possible in plants, where it is found that the gene differences between species that are similar enough to form hybrids are numbered in hundreds rather than in tens or units.

In animals, where hybridization between species is rarely possible, another method of estimating genetic differences can be used. This is to test many different proteins from the species under examination, to find what proportion of proteins have different compositions and therefore different genetic control. If these proteins are regarded as a random sample of all the genes of the organisms, and if one can guess at the total number of genes in the genotype (a procedure that is beset with difficulties), the proportion of protein differences will give a rough estimate of the number of genes in which the two species differ. By this method, two superficially very similar species of *Drosophila* are found to differ in thousands, rather than hundreds, of genes, perhaps 30–40 per cent of the total number of genes. One important conclusion to be drawn from this surprising evidence is that close similarity between two organisms is no guarantee that they have the same genes – the same phenotype, or external appearance, can be the end-product of different genotypes. This emphasizes once again that the phenotype is not the expression of a series of individual genes, but a co-operative effort, the result of interaction between genes.

The magnitude of the genetic difference between outwardly similar species may also seem to be an obstacle to the ideas set out earlier in this section – of gene differences accumulating gradually, as a result of selection in different environments. Surely, to expect thousands of gene differences to accumulate between two populations is asking too much? But the method of protein sampling to estimate genetic differences can also be used on members of different populations of the same species, and on individuals from the same population. These tests give equally surprising results. In man, and in several other widespread vertebrate species, the difference between two individuals from the same population is estimated to involve roughly 6 per cent of the total number of genes. This means that in a man, for instance, the half-set of chromosomes received from each parent will carry different alleles over about 6 per cent of their length. In invertebrate animals, smaller and less mobile than vertebrates, and less insulated from the environment by internal control systems, two individuals from a population may differ in about 15 per cent of their genes. If different populations are compared, for example two races of man, the gene differences are only 1 or 2 per cent higher than those between individuals. If two subspecies are compared, the differences are again greater by a few per cent (Fig. 31).

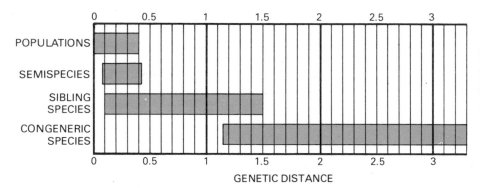

Figure 31
Genetic distance in groups of animals.
The bars show the range in groups with different degrees of relationship. 'Populations' are different geographic groups within one species. 'Semispecies' are populations that may hybridize, like members of the same species, but show behavioural and other differences that limit interbreeding (like the gulls discussed on p. 6). 'Sibling species' behave like different species and do not interbreed, but are so similar that they cannot be distinguished easily (like the *Anopheles* mosquitoes discussed on p. 3). 'Congeneric species' are members of the same genus, such as lion and tiger, or wolf and coyote. The information comes from comparisons of many proteins in insects, crustaceans, fishes, amphibians, reptiles and mammals. The numbers on the scale are the average number of amino acid differences detected in the comparisons, and are roughly equal to the number of mutations fixed in each gene.

Comparisons of this sort lead to two conclusions. First, the number of gene differences between two species, though very large, is not inordinately greater than the difference between individuals of the same species. Second, the scale of genetic difference increases quite gradually and regularly when one compares two individuals, two populations, two subspecies and two species.

Before looking at examples of *speciation* (i.e. species formation), in the next section, it will be as well to summarize the factors, discussed earlier in this section, that should influence the origin of new species. In nature, species are broken up into more or less isolated breeding populations. The greater the geographic spread of a species, the greater the range of environments that it will meet. Environmental changes result in high frequency or fixation, by natural selection, of mutations favourable in the new conditions, so that in widespread species genetic differences between populations will accumulate. How far such genetic changes go will depend on gene flow between the different populations, caused by migration or contacts between the populations, and so on. If there is little or no gene exchange over long periods of time, the gene-pools of two populations may diverge to the point where fertility between them is impaired when they do come into contact. Reduced fertility can arise from a variety of causes – genetic incompatibility, behavioural, seasonal or ecological isolation. It is important to realize that in sexual species reproductive isolation and barriers to fertile crosses are features of populations, not individuals, and can only develop gradually, by change in the genetic constitution of the whole population. Isolating mechanisms cannot arise, like mutations, in one individual, because such an individual would be prevented from breeding (except by self-fertilization) as effectively as if it had developed a lethal mutation.

We should therefore expect new species to result from long-continued isolation of different populations of a species. The most obvious examples of that situation are when populations of a terrestrial species occur on different islands. Rather than select examples from a variety of places, we can look at one group of islands – the Galapagos – in some detail.

101

10 Speciation in the Galapagos Islands

Darwin first became convinced that species can change and divide when, in 1835, he spent five weeks in the Galapagos archipelago, in the Pacific, during the voyage of HMS *Beagle*. The ship had been surveying the coast of South America for more than three years, and during frequent trips ashore Darwin became thoroughly familiar with the fauna and flora of the continent, so that he was ideally prepared for the peculiarities of Galapagos animals and plants.

The Galapagos archipelago is an isolated group of volcanic islands lying on the Equator, about 1000 km (600 miles) east of the South American mainland. The largest island, Albemarle, is about 120 km (75 miles) long, and its highest volcano reaches 1650 m (5400 feet). There are four other fairly large islands, eleven smaller ones, and many small islets and rocks. The large islands have quite a rich flora, zoned according to altitude, with dense, humid forest between about 220 m (750 feet) and 440 m (1500 feet).

10·1   Fauna of the Galapagos

The fauna of the Galapagos, though very peculiar, is clearly related to that of the South American mainland. Darwin wrote 'it was most striking to be surrounded by new birds, new reptiles, new shells, new insects, new plants, and yet by innumerable trifling details of structure, and even by the tones of voice and plumage of the birds, to have the temperate plains of Patagonia, or the hot dry deserts of Northern Chile, vividly brought before my eyes'. He went on to say that the islands are quite different from the South American coast in geological and climatic features, but are very like the Cape Verde islands in the Atlantic. Yet the Galapagos fauna and flora resemble those of South America, not the Cape Verde islands, which have animals and plants of African type.

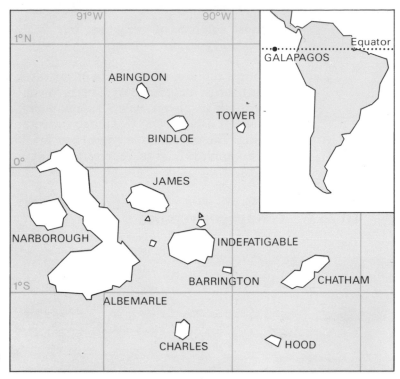

Figure 32
Map of the
Galapagos
archipelago. The
names of the islands
are the old English
ones, used in
Darwin's time and in
the names of many
Galapagos species.
The islands now have
Spanish names.

In the Galapagos, Darwin was particularly impressed by one
fact: 'by far the most remarkable feature in ... this archipelago
... is that the different islands ... are inhabited by a different
set of beings.... I never dreamed that islands, about fifty or
sixty miles apart, and most of them in sight of each other, ...
would have been differently tenanted.' He first noticed this
when he learned that the Vice-Governor of the islands could
tell from which island any giant tortoise had come by features
of its shell. He also took particular notice of a group of land
birds, since called 'Darwin's finches', which vary from island
to island. Since Darwin's time, the islands have been repeat-
edly visited by naturalists, and his opinions of the significance
of the animals and plants have been thoroughly confirmed.
Here there is only space to discuss a few of the animals, and
the reptiles and birds provide good examples.

Looking first at the fauna of the archipelago as a whole, without distinguishing particular islands, the assemblage of animals
is unusual. Until domestic animals were introduced, there
were no mammals except for rats, bats and seals. Land and
water birds are present in some variety and include the north-

ernmost colonies of penguins, but many important South American types are missing.

Amongst reptiles, there are giant tortoises, a few snakes and many lizards, including large, herbivorous iguanas. There are no amphibians (frogs, newts, salamanders, etc.) at all, and no freshwater fishes. Most Galapagos insects are small, drab and retiring. There is only one type of bee, few butterflies or moths, and no aphids, fleas or representatives of many other insect groups.

10·2   Galapagos reptiles

A

The reptiles are amongst the most abundant and interesting Galapagos animals. Taking the giant tortoises first, subsequent work has confirmed the opinion of the Vice-Governor in Darwin's time, that each island has its own variety. The tortoises are the largest native land animals, up to nearly two metres (six feet) long and 270 kg (600 lb) in weight. Galapagos is an old Spanish word for tortoise, and the tortoises attracted early visitors, buccaneers and whalers, to the islands in search of fresh meat. Today, tortoises occur on seven of the islands. On four others they have been exterminated, by man, within the last hundred and fifty years. All these tortoises belong to the same species, *Geochelone elephantopus*, but fifteen subspecies are recognized, differing in the shape, colour and thickness of the shell, length of neck and legs, and in size. Ten islands each have their own peculiar subspecies (four of these are now extinct), while on the largest island, Albemarle, there are five different subspecies, each confined to the neighbourhood of one of the five major volcanoes on the island.

There are two main types of tortoise, one with a domed shell and a short neck (Fig. 33A), and the other with long legs and neck, and a shell that flares up in front, so that the head and neck can be raised (Fig. 33B). The distribution of these two types is associated with habitat – the long-necked forms live on arid islands with much broken ground, where they must raise their heads to feed on shrubs and prickly pear; and the short-necked varieties live on moister islands, where grass and

Figure 33
Galapagos giant tortoises, *Geochelone elephantopus.*
A, a short-necked, domed-shell form from the north of Albemarle Island; an adult male, about a metre long. B, a long-necked, flared-shell form from Abingdon Island; two views of an adult male, about a metre long.

B

other low foliage is available as food. So it seems that some of the differences between the island races are adaptive.

The prickly pear cactus, the principal food of the tortoises, also varies from island to island. On islands where tortoises have never occurred the cacti are low and spreading, with soft spines. But on all the islands where there are tortoises the cacti are erect and tree-like, with stiff spines. The tree-like cacti (four

A

B

106

C

D

different species) seem to have evolved this growth habit in response to browsing by tortoises.

The large iguanas are perhaps the oddest and most characteristic Galapagos reptiles. There are two sorts, land iguanas (*Conolophus*) and marine iguanas (*Amblyrhynchus*) (Fig. 34). Both are large animals, over a metre in length, and are related to South American forms. The land iguanas live in burrows and are mainly herbivorous, although they also eat insects. They are found only on the central group of islands, and there are two species, one restricted to Barrington Island, the other originally present on five islands, but now extinct on two of them. These two island populations have been exterminated in the last century, one by competition from introduced pigs, the other following the establishment of an American air-base during the Second World War.

Marine iguanas are a unique feature of the Galapagos, found nowhere else in the world. These animals spend most of their time on the shore, and enter the sea only to feed. They eat seaweed, clinging to rocks in the surf or swimming down to the bottom in depths of as much as 11 metres, where they can stay nearly an hour without surfacing to breathe. They differ from the land iguanas in having partially webbed toes and a deep, flat-sided tail, used in swimming. They have been seen up to a kilometre out at sea, but rarely go so far from land. Marine iguanas occur on all the islands, and all these populations are included in a single species. But there are differences between island populations, especially on the remote southern and northern islands, in colour, behaviour and size.

Small lizards, called lava lizards (*Tropidurus*), are found on all the islands except three remote northern ones (Fig. 35). There are seven different species of these lizards, differing in colour, size, shape, scale pattern, and so on, and on each of the twelve islands where lizards are found, there is only one species. *Tropidurus albemarlensis* occupies the central group of four islands and two other small ones. Each of the other six species is confined to one island. Amongst the six different island populations of *T. albemarlensis*, the display behaviour is characteristic for each island, indicating some evolutionary divergence.

10·3 Galapagos birds

Galapagos birds include several species which are found elsewhere, and which show no local differentiation in the archipelago. This category contains sea birds (terns, petrels, frigate-birds, etc.) and some land birds (cuckoo, moorhen). There are other widespread species which have developed a local sub-species in the Galapagos – a pelican, a tern, two herons, a duck, a flamingo and two owls. In other cases, the Galapagos form is sufficiently distinct to be named as a local species, as

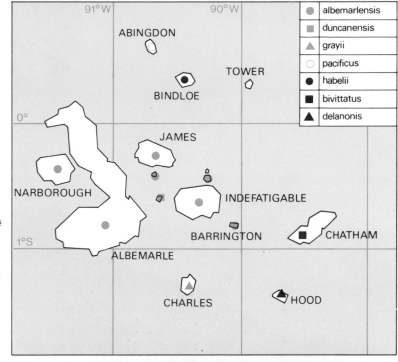

●	albemarlensis
■	duncanensis
▲	grayii
○	pacificus
●	habelii
■	bivittatus
▲	delanonis

Figure 35
Above, the distribution of the species of lava lizards (*Tropidurus*) in the Galapagos. Below, a lava lizard, *Tropidurus albemarlensis*, behind a marine iguana on the shore of Narborough Island (photo Dr J. E. P. Whittaker).

is the albatross, the penguin, a gull and the hawk. Some Galapagos birds are so different that they are placed in a special genus (see section 11·1), such as the peculiar flightless cormorant, a nocturnal gull and the Galapagos dove. None of the birds mentioned so far has evolved island varieties within the archipelago. Local differentiation is found especially in two groups of birds – the mocking birds, a Galapagos genus with

109

Figure 36
Darwin's finches.
On the left, a tree
finch, *Camarhynchus
psittacula*. It has a
short, thick beak, and
feeds mainly on
beetles and similar
insects taken from the
bark of trees. On the
right, the cactus
ground finch,
Geospiza scandens. It
has a long, slender
beak, and feeds
mainly on the flowers
of prickly pear cactus,
as shown in the
picture. Natural size,
from John Gould's
plates in *Zoology of
the Voyage of the
Beagle* (1841).

Figure 37
The heads of four
species of Darwin's
finches, from Charles
Darwin's *Journal of
Researches* (1845).

1. Large ground finch,
   Geospiza magnirostris.
2. Medium ground finch,
   Geospiza fortis.
3. Insectivorous tree finch,
   Camarhynchus parvulus.
4. Warbler finch,
   Certhidea olivacea.

four species, and Darwin's finches, a distinct subfamily containing five genera and a total of fifteen species.

The four species of mocking birds (thrush-sized, predatory birds) are distributed in the same way as some of the reptiles – no island has more than one species, three of the species are each confined to one outlying southern island, and the fourth occurs on all the other islands and has seven subspecies, most of the remote islands having one subspecies each.

Darwin's finches are the commonest land birds in the Galapagos. They are mostly sparrow-sized, and are all dull in colour. The different genera and species are recognized mainly by differences in the shape of the beak (Figs 36, 37) and in feeding habits. One group, the ground finches, contains six species which live in the coastal zone and the lowlands, and feed mainly on the ground, on seeds and insects. The species differ in the shape of the beak, and in the size and toughness of the seeds on which each specializes. One species has a long, curved beak and feeds on the flowers of prickly pear cacti. A second group, the tree finches, contains three species with large, parrot-like beaks. They live in the forest zone, feeding in the trees on insects and seeds. The warbler finch, placed in a genus of its own, has a slender beak and feeds only on insects, sometimes taken on the wing. Another species, also placed in a genus of its own, is the vegetarian tree finch, a larger bird living in the forest zone and feeding on fruit, buds and soft seeds. Finally, there is a fifth genus containing two species with habits like woodpeckers, feeding on insects taken from tree trunks and branches. Unlike woodpeckers, they do not have strong, sharply-pointed beaks and long tongues, but they make up for this by using twigs or cactus spines as tools, to poke insects out of crevices. One of these birds, the mangrove finch, ranges up into the forest zone.

Darwin's finches show a wide range of feeding habits. Their distribution in the archipelago is unlike that of the reptiles and mocking birds, where each island has only one species or subspecies of a particular animal. Each island usually has several species of finch, and there are twelve islands with seven or more species. Only one finch species is confined to a single island, and one other species is found only on two islands. The finch fauna of an island will contain representatives of different groups of finches, rather than several species of the same type. The ground finches and the warbler finch are the most widespread, occurring on all the islands. Tree finches and the vegetarian tree finch are missing from the outlying islands to the south and north, and the tool-using finches are restricted to the central group of islands. Within the more widely-distributed species there is local differentiation of island subspecies, differing in song, behaviour and other details.

10·4   Galapagos history and species

Before summarizing the evidence from Galapagos reptiles and birds on the process of speciation, it is worth considering how, and when, the archipelago became populated. As volcanoes, some of them still active, the islands evidently came out of the sea comparatively recently, and would have had no flora or fauna when they first emerged. When the continents were thought to be fixed, it was natural to assume that the Galapagos and the American mainland had been in the same places since the islands first appeared, and that animals and plants reached the islands from the mainland by rare accidents. The South Equatorial current flows from the South American coast to the islands, and could have carried floating objects – seeds, animals, rafts of vegetation. Galapagos tortoises float, and some have survived several days at sea. Lizards and snakes or their eggs might be transported on tree trunks, or mats of vegetation. The trade winds also blow from the mainland to the islands, and might help stray birds on their way. The traditional view is that the islands were colonized like this, by the chance arrival of perhaps a single pair of one species, or a single fertilized female of another.

But according to the modern theory of continental drift (Fig. 38), or *plate tectonics*, the crust of the earth consists of a number of rigid plates, some of them bearing continents, which are in constant motion relative to one another, and may grow by the generation of new crust at mid-ocean ridges, or shrink by the consumption of old crust at ocean trenches. Two geographic features will be in relative motion unless they are on the same plate. The Galapagos islands lie close to the junction of three plates, in an area of crust generation and complex motion. The islands are the product of a volcanic hot-spot at this junction. The hot-spot has been active for thirty to forty million years, but the islands seem to be only one or two mil-

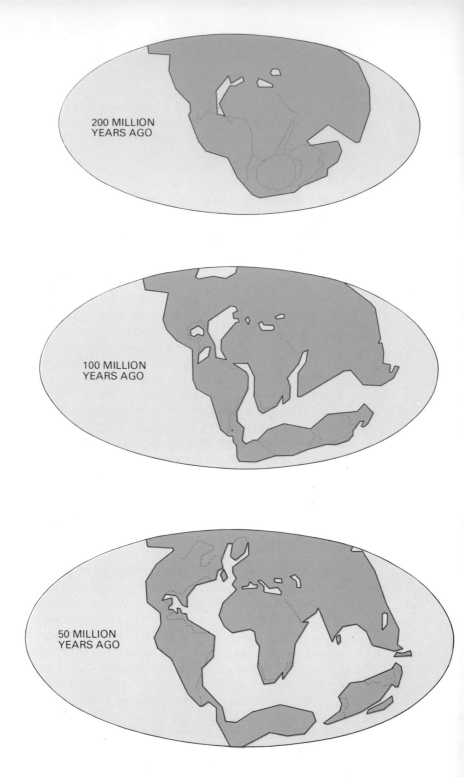

200 MILLION YEARS AGO

100 MILLION YEARS AGO

50 MILLION YEARS AGO

lion years old. The existing islands are probably only the latest of a series of archipelagos, successively erupting, moving away from the hot-spot, and being eroded away. These earlier islands may also have been closer to the American mainland. So we cannot say how or when the present inhabitants of the islands arrived. Darwin's finches may be the descendants of a single pair of birds, blown, by chance, from the mainland; or they may be the descendants of one or more finch populations on some earlier island or islands, closer to the mainland.

Luckily, it is not necessary to know how or when each element of the present Galapagos fauna arrived before we can draw some inferences, of general validity, about how new species arise. The water between the archipelago and the South American mainland is an effective barrier, as is shown by the absence of amphibians and large mammals, although there are habitats suitable for both. The water between the islands is also an effective barrier, even to some birds, which are physically quite capable of the crossing, but do not occupy all islands with suitable habitats. In the archipelago as a whole, some species (insects, birds, reptiles) are the same as on the mainland. Others are differentiated into Galapagos subspecies or species, or are sufficiently divergent to be placed in a Galapagos genus. The same effects are seen within the archipelago – populations on different islands may be different species, as in the lava lizards and mocking birds, but the giant tortoises have only diverged into subspecies, and the land iguanas have hardly diverged at all on most islands. So isolation does not invariably produce new species, but we cannot say if this is because some island populations have not been separated for long enough, or because chance migration from island to island maintains gene exchange between populations, or because the islands are so similar that no adaptive change is selected, or if others factors are involved. The remoteness of some of the islands seems to be correlated with differentiation of their inhabitants, but the greater uniformity of the fauna of the central group of islands could be an indication that they were linked by dry land in quite recent times, and have only been separated by subsidence or changes in sea-level.

Some of the divergence between island forms is obviously adaptive, as in the long-legged and long-necked tortoises, the differences between land and marine iguanas, and especially in the adaptations of the different groups of finches. These

115

finches are an excellent example of *adaptive radiation*, where one type of animal or plant gives rise to a variety of forms adapted to different ways of life. Why have the finches of South America, or Great Britain for that matter, not developed a range of adaptations like the Galapagos finches? The reason must be that British finches are unable to produce warbler-like or woodpecker-like forms because those ways of life, or *ecological niches*, are already filled, by warblers and wood-peckers. This emphasizes the fact that an important agent in natural selection is competition between different species for the limited resources of the environment. The same point is illustrated by the adaptations of Galapagos tortoises and prickly pears. On islands where tortoises occur, filling the niche of large herbivores (occupied on the American mainland by large mammals), the prickly pears have responded by developing stiff spines and a tree-like form.

The finches raise one problem of speciation. They are almost the only Galapagos animal group in which one island may contain several species. Is it possible that these different species diverged on one island? This is a question that has led to long discussions – whether geographic isolation of populations is always necessary before species can diverge, or whether they can split in one place. It is not necessary to go into the details of these arguments here. The problem is analogous to the spread of an advantageous mutation, discussed in section 7·3. Suppose, to take an extreme example, that one member of a finch population hit on the idea of using a thorn to dig insects out of tree bark. It could perhaps teach its offspring the same trick, and in turn they might teach their offspring. Could a new species, in which the tool-using habit was genetically fixed, arise in this way? Only if the first tool-using finches were much more likely to mate with birds having the same habit. This might come about if the tool-using finches fed and mated in the trees, while the ancestral non-tool-using population fed and mated on the ground, perhaps in more open country. But this is, in effect, geographic isolation, though on a small scale.

Nearly all supposed examples of speciation within an originally undivided population seem to hinge on small scale geographic, or ecological, isolation like this. So speciation in Galapagos finches could, in theory, have been initiated within one island population. But the examples of mocking birds and the various reptiles, where one island always has only one species or subspecies, makes it more probable that the finch species diverged in the same way, on different islands. If so, the present situation, where several species of finch may occur on one island, is due to reinvasion by the finches, each species spreading through the archipelago from its original island home. The fact that two or more species of finch can co-exist in the same habitat is evidence that they have developed effective reproductive isolation, preventing gene exchange between them. It is also an indication that they have different habits, because if they had exactly the same ecological requirements they would be in direct competition, and one would surely be more efficient at finding those requirements than another, which would eventually become extinct.

There is one more general question about the origin of species. In choosing the Galapagos as an example, and concentrating on the land animals there, I have cheated. For the environment open to those animals is broken up into separate islands, and it is easy to imagine how two new species may develop, through isolation and divergence, on two islands. Looking back to the origin of these two island populations, we would have to guess that at first the animals lived only on one island, and that, by chance, one, two or a few individuals reached the second island: the new species represents the descendants of these colonizers. Is this a valid model of how new species originate? It may be so on an archipelago, but in a more uniform environment, like the ocean or the American prairies, we might imagine a different model, in which a large population was divided by the slow development of a new geographical or ecological barrier. These two alternative models are shown diagrammatically in Figure 39. In the upper diagrams, the process of speciation is gradual, involves large populations, and there is no decisive moment or event in the origin of the two new species. In the lower model, the parent species remains unchanged, and the new species originates rapidly following a particular event, like the arrival of a founder population of lizards on a new island, or of insects on a different species of food plant. Under these conditions – a new environment and a small population – change might be very rapid. The new environment will exert new selective forces, or if it is uninhabited, selection may be relaxed as the population expands to fill the empty niche. The small original population will mean inbreeding, and so rapid fixation of genes, by natural selection or by genetic drift. In these circumstances a 'genetic revolution' could occur, and a new species, infertile with the parent species, might develop in a few generations.

These two models of speciation are not mutually exclusive. The gradual model (the one favoured by Darwin) might prevail in rather uniform environments, and the rapid, revolutionary one (called *quantum speciation*) in fluctuating or 'patchy' environments, and intermediates between the two can be imagined. Examples can be found to fit each model, and each has its devotees. But the fact is that no one has actually observed the origin of even one new species in nature, and we cannot tell if the gradual or quantum model is the dominant one.

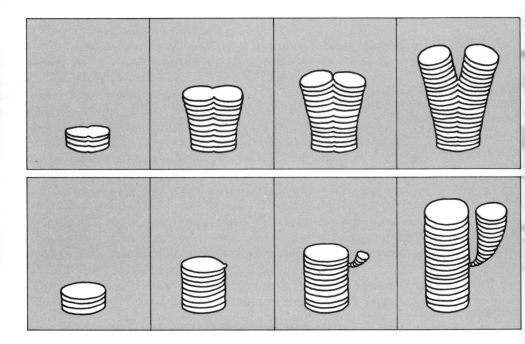

Figure 39

Alternative models of the origin of new species. The shapes represent the entire population of a species, with time indicated by upward growth. In the upper series of diagrams, a species splits into two roughly equal daughter-species, which gradually diverge and differentiate. In the lower series, a small population differentiates rapidly, and develops into a successful new species, while the parent species remains unchanged. In this second model, we should imagine that the 'trunk' is continually budding off 'twigs' – small, divergent populations – most of which die out or merge back into the 'trunk'.

A final point about Darwin's finches, the most diverse Galapagos group, is that they illustrate what might be called 'rounds of speciation'. Their diversity exists on at least three levels: between the main groups (genera) such as ground finches and tree finches; within each group, as between the six species of ground finch; and within each species, as between the island subspecies of a single widespread ground finch. These three levels must be regarded as the product of three successive, and continuous, rounds or episodes of divergence, initiated by the splitting of one original species. This idea, of a hierarchy of species splits, is explored further in the next chapter.

11 Evolution beyond the species level

I cannot doubt that the theory of descent with modification embraces all the members of the same great class or kingdom.

Charles Darwin

The Galapagos archipelago gives many examples of speciation. Equally good examples can be found in other parts of the world: in Britain and its offshore islands, in the sea on either side of the isthmus of Panama, and so on. But all such examples illustrate change and divergence on a relatively trivial level. It is reasonable to ask whether small-scale changes like these can possibly account for large-scale differences like those between a man and a mouse, or an elephant and an oak tree. And could the selection of small, favourable mutations account for the perfection of a peacock's tail, or a hawk's eye, or the human brain? There are three main lines of approach to these questions – through the classification of animals and plants, fossils and the geological history of the world, and the newer field of molecular evolution.

11·1 Classification

And thus, the forms of life throughout the universe become divided into groups subordinate to groups.   Charles Darwin

Darwin found one of the strongest arguments for his theory in the fact that animal and plant species fall into groups, and that these groups form a nested series or hierarchy, smaller groups or sets of species (such as owls and ducks, or seals and deer) being included within successively larger groups (birds and mammals within vertebrates, vertebrates and invertebrates within animals, etc.). Observations like this have certainly been made since antiquity, but the system of classification now in use in biology is based on the work of the eighteenth-century Swedish naturalist Linnaeus (Fig. 56).

Linnaeus introduced binomial names, giving each species two Latin or latinized names, of which the first (genus name) is a group name which may be shared by several species, while the second (trivial name) is particular and identifies the individual species. For example, the Linnaean genus *Turdus* contains several British species, including *Turdus merula*, the blackbird; *T. philomelos*, the song thrush; *T. viscivorus*, the mistle thrush; *T. pilaris*, the fieldfare; and *T. torquatus*, the ring ouzel. Just as species are grouped in a genus, genera may be grouped in a category or set of higher rank, the family (*Turdus* is grouped with robins, nightingales, redstarts, etc., in a subfamily Turdinae, which in turn is placed in the family Muscicapidae, including other subfamilies for warblers, flycatchers and tits), families may be grouped in orders (the order Passeriformes contains all perching birds), orders in classes (the class Aves contains all birds), classes in a phylum (e.g. phylum Vertebrata), and phyla in a kingdom (e.g. kingdom Animalia).

When he introduced this system, Linnaeus intended it partly as a convenient aid to the memory, a means of making comprehensible the diversity of nature. He recognized about 12 000 species of plants and animals, grouped in about a thousand genera, and expected the educated man to be able to remember the genera (today species are numbered in millions, and genera in hundreds of thousands). From this point of view – convenience – the Linnaean system hardly differs from other hierarchical classifications, such as those used in libraries, where books are divided by topics and subtopics, and each subgroup is further broken down by size, and then by alphabetical order of authors. But Linnaeus also had a higher purpose than merely to catalogue nature. He believed that he was uncovering the plan of the Creator, since he thought that species were fixed and individually created. (Later in life Linnaeus seems to have decided that species might change and that God could originally have created only the genera.)

Linnaeus and his successors recognized genera, families and other categories on the basis of similarities in structure, and believed that each group had a set of features which were its essence, or ideal plan, corresponding to something in the mind of the Creator. The science of comparative anatomy developed as a means of searching out these ideal plans, or archetypes. The central concept of comparative anatomy is *homology*, a

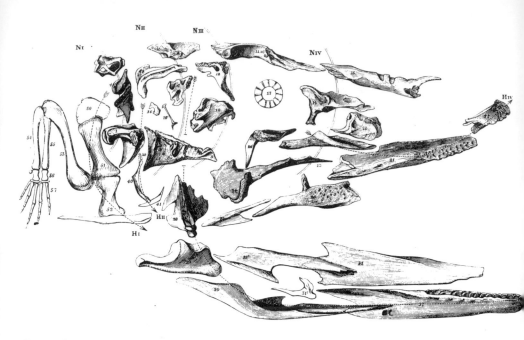

Figure 40
Homology.
The skull and forelimb skeleton of a crocodile (above) and an ostrich (opposite) 'exploded' to show the separate bones, with homologous bones marked by numbers. By comparing the skeletons of many different vertebrates (fishes, reptiles, birds, mammals), Richard Owen deduced the imaginary animal shown below, his concept of the archetype or lowest common denominator of vertebrates. A modern evolutionist would construct a different imaginary animal, and call it the common ancestor of vertebrates. From Owen's *Homologies of the Vertebrate Skeleton* (1848).

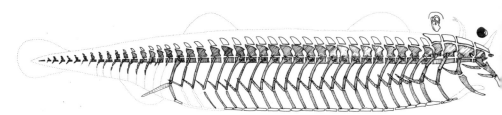

term introduced by Sir Richard Owen (Figs 67, 68), the first director of the British Museum (Natural History), London, and a powerful anti-evolutionist. Homology is the name given to the relationship between, for example, the arm of a man, the front leg of a horse, the wing of a bat or bird, and the flipper of a dolphin or turtle; or between our fingernails, the claws of a cat and the hooves of a horse or cow (Fig. 40). Homologous structures may differ in function or composition, but they correspond in relative position, and in the embryonic

development of each individual they arise from similar precursors. (In genetics, the word homology is used in a slightly different sense, for chromosomes or parts of chromosomes that correspond in structure and pair in meiosis; see p. 25).

By the time Darwin published *The Origin*, Linnaean hierarchical classification and classical comparative anatomy – the search for the archetype of each group by identifying homologous structures – were highly developed. Darwin was the first to suggest, by detailed argument, the significance of the natural hierarchy: that the relationship between the species of a genus, or the members of a family, is 'blood' relationship, caused by descent, and divergence, from a common ancestor. This is shown diagrammatically in Figure 41. The Linnaean classification can be shown in a form resembling a family tree or genealogy, and the Darwinian interpretation is that a classification based on similarities and differences between species might accurately reflect the relationships of common ancestry between them. As Darwin wrote, 'our classifications will come to be, as far as they can be so made, genealogies; and will then truly give what may be called the plan of creation'.

As the theory of evolution became accepted, comparative anatomy received a new impetus, for the unravelling of homologies could now be seen as a key to understanding the course of evolution, and 'archetypes' could be replaced by 'common ancestors'. A series of variations in some homologous structure, such as the vertebrate forelimb or skull, leads to the idea of the transformation of the ancestral (or primitive) structure into a variety of divergent, more advanced, or specialized, or derived conditions, each characteristic of a group of species. But Darwin's expectation, that this would result in genealogical classifications, has not yet been fully realized. This may be partly due to inertia and respect for tradition in biologists, but it is also because today, as in Linnaeus's time, classifications have two purposes – to express evolutionary relationships, and to act as *aides-mémoire* or simple summaries of knowledge. These two aims come into conflict, because relationships of common ancestry are almost invariably more complicated than the relationships of similarity and

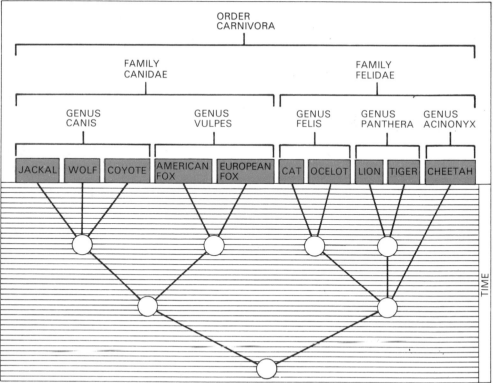

Figure 41
Classification and evolution.
The boxed names are living species, and the brackets and names above show how they are classified in the Linnaean hierarchy. The lower part of the diagram shows a Darwinian interpretation of this classification: the relationships between the species are due to descent from ancestral species (open circles), more or less remote in time.

124

difference on which Linnaean classification is based (see Fig. 42).

In evolutionary biology, the concept 'similarity' or 'resemblance' has three components. One is superficial, non-homologous resemblance caused by convergent evolution (for example, the similar body form of a fish, a whale, a penguin and a seal); a second is resemblance due to retention of unchanged ancestral, primitive homologies (such as the five toes of a frog, a lizard, a hedgehog and a man, whereas horses have one toe, deer and cattle two, rhinoceroses three, birds and dinosaurs four, snakes and whales none); and thirdly, there is similarity in advanced or derived homologous features (like loss of the tail in apes and men). In traditional classification, similarity thought to be due to convergence is disregarded, but the other two types of similarity are used. In genealogical classification, resemblance in primitive, ancestral features is disregarded. Taking the example just mentioned – the five toes of men, hedgehogs, lizards and frogs – this feature tells us that all these animals are related by common ancestry and belong to a group comprising four-footed, five-toed vertebrates. For at that level, a five-toed foot is an advanced feature, when compared with the fins of fishes. But if we want to know whether a lizard or a hedgehog is more closely related to men or frogs, the fact that they all have a similar foot is no longer any help, and we have to look for other more restricted homologies.

It is found that lizards, hedgehogs and men develop from an embryo which becomes enclosed in a special membrane, the amnion. This is an advanced feature that allows reptiles, birds and mammals to breed on dry land, and differentiates them from frogs and fishes, whose eggs must be laid in water. Going on to compare lizards, hedgehogs and men, we find that hedgehogs and men are warm-blooded, only replace their teeth once, have hair, and other homologous features that relate them and differentiate them from lizards. By procedures like this, relying on homologies that characterize different groups and subgroups, it is possible to work out the genealogical relationships of most plants and animals in some detail, and to arrive at a classification which implies splitting of ancestral species into daughter-species whose descendants are now groups which are each other's closest relatives.

These relationships often demonstrate that traditional groups, like fishes and reptiles, which appeared to be as 'natural' to early evolutionists as they did to Linnaeus, are 'unnatural' in a genealogical sense, because they include species whose relationships lie elsewhere. This is demonstrated in Figure 42, where the traditional classification of the main vertebrate groups is contrasted with the much more complex classification dictated by the relationships of common ancestry.

Whether or not biologists should follow Darwin's advice, and

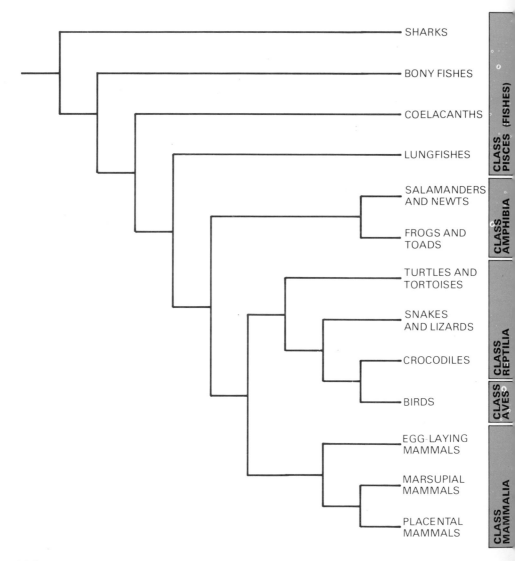

make their classifications genealogical, is still controversial. The decision rests on a choice between a traditional classification whose main virtue is that it is stable and easily memorized; and a more complicated classification, changing with new discoveries, whose main virtue is that it is a scientific theory of relationships. However the choice is made, the fact remains that the basis for a genealogical classification exists, in the unravelling of homologies.

The relevance of this to the theory of evolution is that homologous features are found at every level of diversity, from those that unite two subspecies of Galapagos reptiles, to those that unite all vertebrates, or all multicellular animals, or all living organisms (like the universal system of coding genetic information in DNA). The resulting hierarchical classification of all organisms is a clear indication that the causes which produce the divergence between Galapagos species and subspecies also operated in the remote past, causing divergence within extinct species which were ancestral to different major groups, such as lungfishes and land vertebrates, or sharks and other jawed vertebrates, or plants and animals.

11·2 Fossils and geology

Fossils are the remains of long-dead organisms, preserved, by natural burial, in the rocks of the earth's crust. With rare exceptions, all that is preserved is the hard parts or skeleton. But, where the skeleton is moulded to the various parts of the organism, as in land plants, crustaceans, insects and vertebrates, the fossil may yield a great deal of information about its original owner.

Figure 42
Vertebrate relationships. The diagram shows current opinions on the genealogical relationships between the main groups of vertebrate animals. On the right are the classes named in traditional classifications. In the genealogical tree, the groups are indicated by vertical bars: only two of these (Amphibia, Mammalia) correspond with traditional vertebrate classes.

When animals and plants die, their remains are normally eaten by predators and scavengers, and eventually broken down by micro-organisms. Fossilization – where the remains escape these hazards and are buried by sediment – is therefore a rare occurrence, and requires unusual conditions. The chance that a fossil, once formed, will be found is even more remote, for only a minute proportion of fossil-bearing rocks are accessible to us, others having been eroded away, buried deep beneath the continents or oceans by earth movements, or consumed at the margins of shrinking tectonic plates. Darwin devoted two chapters of *The Origin* to fossils, but spent the whole of the first in saying how imperfect the geological record of life is. For it seemed obvious to him that, if his theory of evolution is correct, fossils ought to provide incontrovertible proof of it, since each stratum should contain links between the species of earlier and later strata, and if sufficient fossils were collected, it would be possible to arrange them in ancestor-descendent sequences, and so build up a precise picture of the course of evolution. This was not so in Darwin's time, and today, after more than another hundred years of assiduous fossil collecting, the picture still has extensive gaps.

The other objection that Darwin wished to counter concerned the age of the earth. At that time, many editions of the Bible carried a marginal chronology, calculated from the genealogies of the prophets by a seventeenth-century archbishop, which placed the creation of the world in 4004 BC. The gradual changes that Darwin envisaged as causing the present diversity of species would clearly require a period of time vastly greater than that. Darwin and other nineteenth-century scientists attempted to calculate the age of the earth from the thickness of the sedimentary rocks, the salt content of the oceans, or the heat loss of the sun. Darwin arrived at an estimate of 200–400 million years for the age of the earth. He felt that even this vast period might be too short to account for evolution, but pointed out that we can hardly comprehend the meaning of millions of years.

During the twentieth century, reliable methods of estimating the age of rock samples became available with the discovery of radioactivity. Radioactive elements are unstable, and decay at a rate which is constant for each type of atom. If a newly formed mineral containing a radioactive element is embedded in rock, the products of radioactive decay will also be trapped, and the proportions of the element and its decay products will give an approximate age for the rock. The elements commonly used are uranium and thorium, decaying to produce lead and helium, radioactive potassium producing argon, rubidium producing strontium, and, in comparatively recent rocks (up to about 50 000 years old), radioactive carbon.

*That different strata contain different fossils is evidence of change in the past, but it is not direct evidence of evolution, or of the causes of evolution. Opponents of evolution have used fossils to support their own theories.

Real ages of particular rocks, calculated from radioactive assays, can be combined with the traditional geological time-scale, derived from the fact that strata can be correlated by the fossils they contain,* and that younger strata lie on top of older strata, to give a time-scale of earth history as shown in Figure 43. This enormous period of time is surely sufficient to meet any objections, and we can come back to the question of whether fossils, within this time-scale, provide a picture consonant with evolution. In broad terms, they do. Figure 43 also shows the range in time of the main groups of organisms, and the proportion of subgroups recognizable at different times. The curve for the subgroups shows a regular decrease with increasing age, and in the main groups there is an orderly progression: those which are simplest in organization, like bacteria and simple seaweeds, appear before more highly-organized things like fungi and worms, and these, in turn, appear before seed (flowering) plants or land vertebrates. Thus the fossil record demonstrates progression in geological time, whether progression is defined as the development and further modification of homologous features, or as increase in information content of DNA.

The fossil record is also consonant with evolution in an ecological sense – plants appear before animals (animals must depend on plants for food); land plants appear before land animals; plants with insect-pollinated flowers appear after insects, and so on.

There is a third way in which fossils do not contradict the theory of evolution. We saw in the last section that living species fall into a hierarchical classification, and that evolution leads us to believe that this hierarchy of groups of different rank reflects genealogy – divergence from ancestral species in the more or less remote past. If this is correct, we should expect fossils to fit into the same system. Fossils from later (more recent) geological epochs should be members of living groups of low rank, and fossils from remote periods should only fit into groups of high rank. This is indeed so – for example, the genealogy of living vertebrate groups shown in Figure 42 can be filled out by the addition of fossils, as in Figure 44, the fossils providing a real time-scale for the various branching points, and a check on the accuracy of the genealogy. As would be expected, we find that advanced groups, like birds, appear later than groups like turtles and amphibians, which in turn appear later than the various types of fishes. Within each group we find the same sort of confirmation: no living mammalian family is recognizable before the late Cretaceous, no living mammalian order before the early Cretaceous, and as

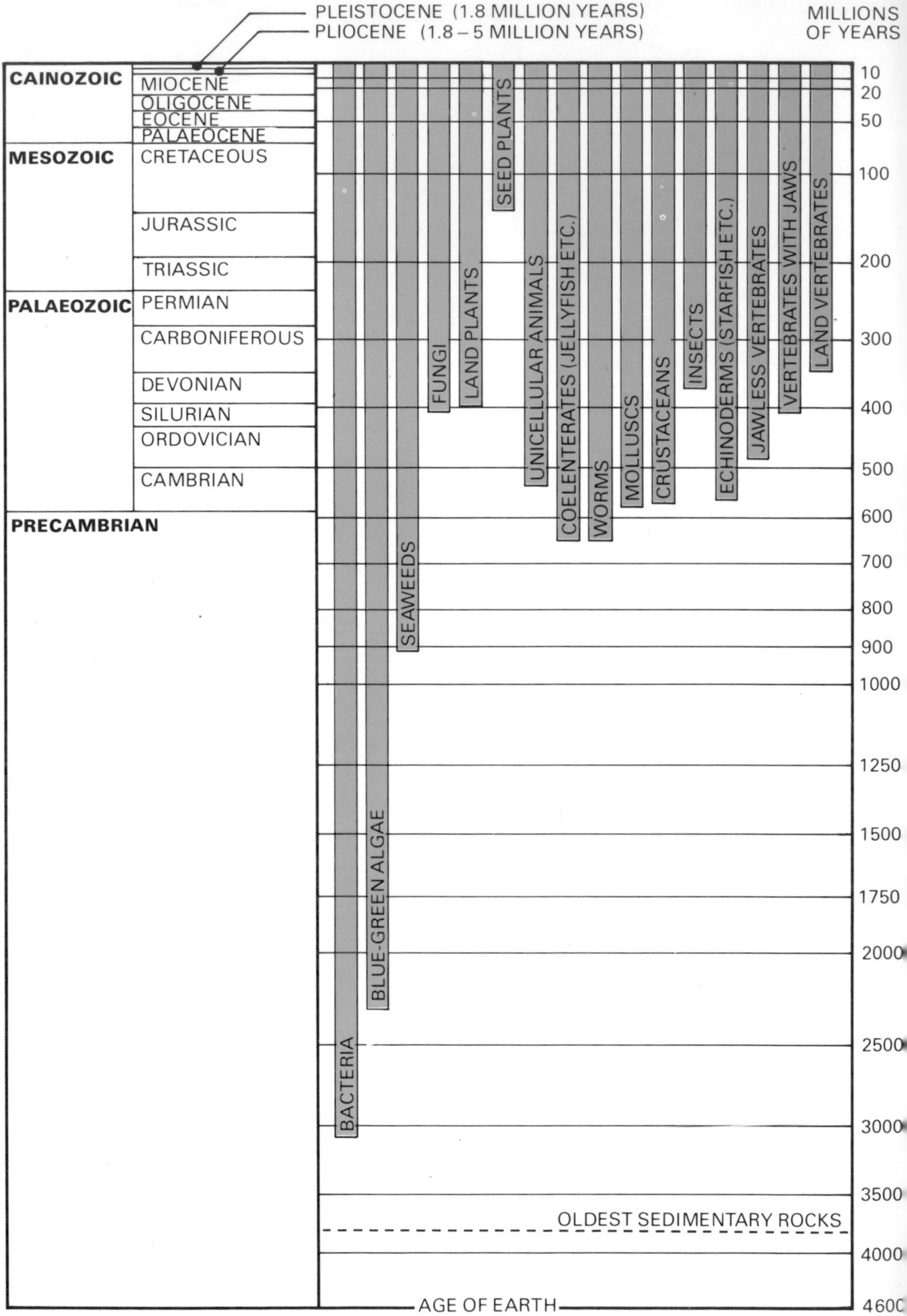

PLEISTOCENE (1.8 MILLION YEARS)
PLIOCENE (1.8 – 5 MILLION YEARS)
MILLIONS OF YEARS
CAINOZOIC
MIOCENE
OLIGOCENE
EOCENE
PALAEOCENE
MESOZOIC
CRETACEOUS
JURASSIC
TRIASSIC
PALAEOZOIC
PERMIAN
CARBONIFEROUS
DEVONIAN
SILURIAN
ORDOVICIAN
CAMBRIAN
PRECAMBRIAN
BACTERIA
BLUE-GREEN ALGAE
SEAWEEDS
FUNGI
LAND PLANTS
SEED PLANTS
UNICELLULAR ANIMALS
COELENTERATES (JELLYFISH ETC.)
WORMS
MOLLUSCS
CRUSTACEANS
INSECTS
ECHINODERMS (STARFISH ETC.)
JAWLESS VERTEBRATES
VERTEBRATES WITH JAWS
LAND VERTEBRATES
10
20
50
100
200
300
400
500
600
700
800
900
1000
1250
1500
1750
2000
2500
3000
3500
OLDEST SEDIMENTARY ROCKS
4000
AGE OF EARTH
4600

Jurassic mammals are followed back they become less diverse and less abundant.

Finally, there is a point made by Darwin, that all fossils fit into the same hierarchy as living species: although we find fossil remains of many bizarre or unexpected extinct groups, none is entirely novel and all can be fitted into the hierarchy of living species at some level.

In several animal and plant groups, enough fossils are known to bridge the wide gaps between existing types. In mammals,

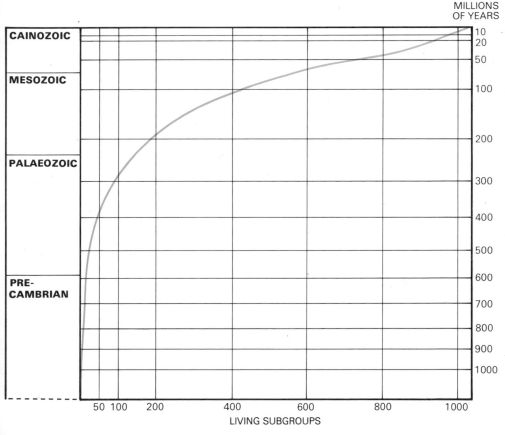

Figure 43
The geological time-scale and a summary of the fossil record. In the chart opposite the names of the geological eras and periods are on the left, and on the right is a scale in millions of years (the scale is logarithmic, giving greater space to more recent times). The vertical bars show the known range in time of the main groups of organisms. The graph above summarizes the time-range of more than a thousand subgroups of organisms. The curve is based on the earliest fossil occurrence of each. About half of them extend back into the Mesozoic (70 million years or more), but only a handful are found in the Precambrian.

131

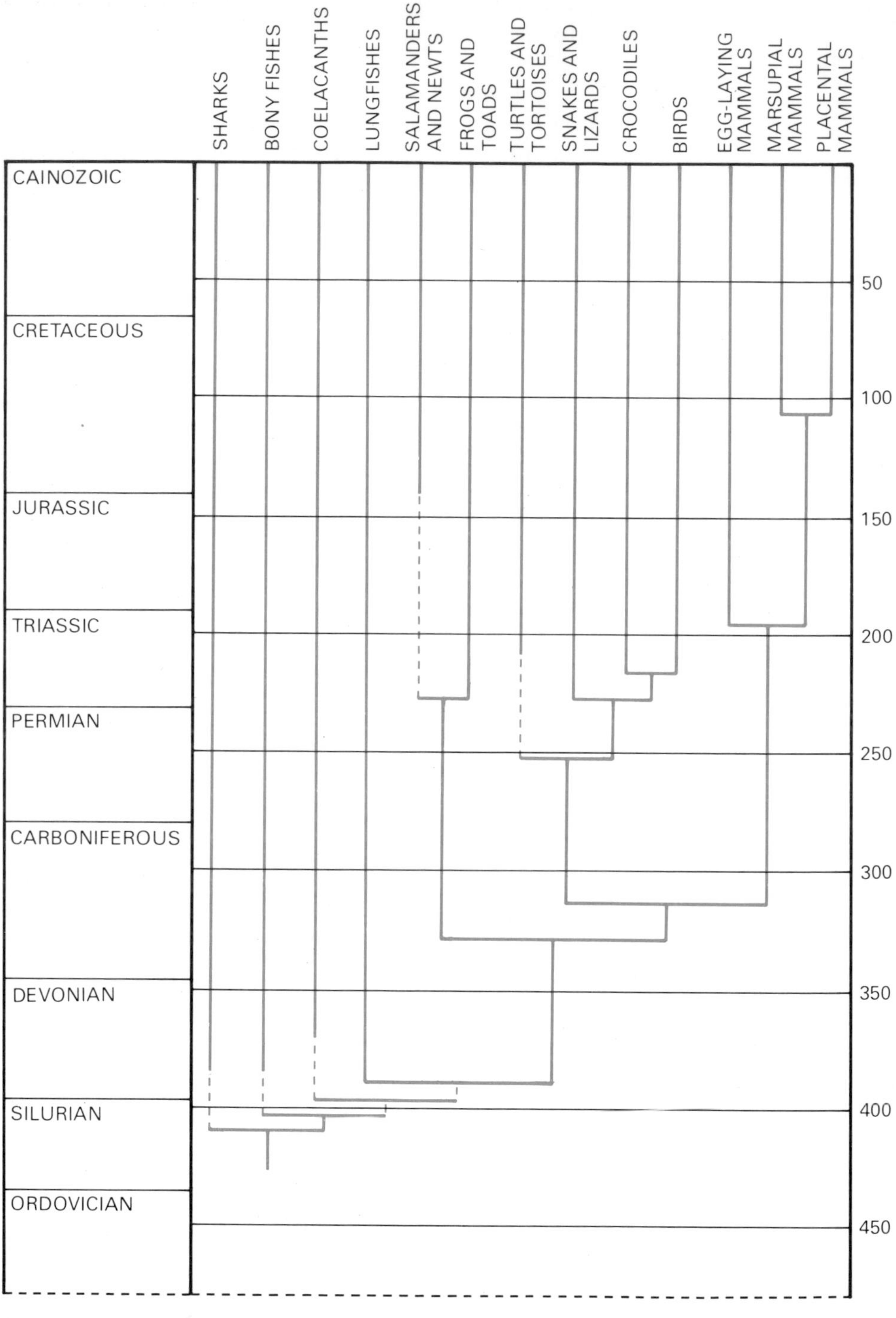
SHARKS
BONY FISHES
COELACANTHS
LUNGFISHES
SALAMANDERS AND NEWTS
FROGS AND TOADS
TURTLES AND TORTOISES
SNAKES AND LIZARDS
CROCODILES
BIRDS
EGG-LAYING MAMMALS
MARSUPIAL MAMMALS
PLACENTAL MAMMALS
CAINOZOIC
CRETACEOUS
JURASSIC
TRIASSIC
PERMIAN
CARBONIFEROUS
DEVONIAN
SILURIAN
ORDOVICIAN
50
100
150
200
250
300
350
400
450

Figure 44
The vertebrate fossil record.
The genealogical tree of vertebrate groups (Fig. 42) can be fitted to the geological time-scale. Solid vertical lines show groups known by fossils; dotted lines indicate 'gaps' in the fossil record – periods when the group is inferred to have existed, but no fossils have been found. These gaps might be due to failures in fossilization, or to mistakes in the genealogy, or to wrongly identified fossils; or they could be (and have been) taken to show that the theory of evolution is wrong.

for example, the gap between horses, asses and zebras (genus *Equus*) and their closest living relatives, the rhinoceroses and tapirs, is filled by an extensive series of fossils extending back sixty million years to a small animal, *Hyracotherium*, which can only be distinguished from the rhinoceros–tapir group by one or two horse-like details of the skull. There are many other examples of fossil 'missing links', such as *Archaeopteryx*, the Jurassic bird which links birds with dinosaurs (Fig. 45), and *Ichthyostega*, the late Devonian amphibian which links land vertebrates and the extinct choanate (having internal nostrils) fishes. But there are still great gaps in the fossil record. Most of the major groups of animals (phyla) appear fully fledged in the early Cambrian rocks (Fig. 43), and we know of no fossil forms linking them. Many different 'explanations' of this have been proposed – that the animals in question were soft-bodied and would not be fossilized; that they lived in places where fossil-bearing rocks were not formed; that the early stages in the evolution of major groups are passed through very rapidly in small populations, and so on. Perhaps the simplest explanation is that in many cases we simply do not yet know what to look for, or how to recognize it if we found it. Fossils may tell us many things, but one thing they can never disclose is whether they were ancestors of anything else.

11·3   Molecular evolution

In the last twenty years, following the discovery that the messages in the genetic code concern protein structure, and the development of methods for analysing the amino acid sequence of protein chains, a new means of investigating evolution has appeared. This involves comparing the structural details of homologous proteins and other molecules in different species. The ultimate aim of this branch of biology must be direct comparison of the base-sequences in the DNA molecules of different species. Rapid methods of sequencing DNA have now been developed, but it has not yet proved possible to apply them to the comparison of higher organisms. That comparison can sometimes be made at second hand, by translating amino acid sequences into the genetic code, and so reconstructing the DNA sequence responsible for them. Various proteins have been investigated in this way, especially cytochromes – molecules which play a part in oxygen metabol-

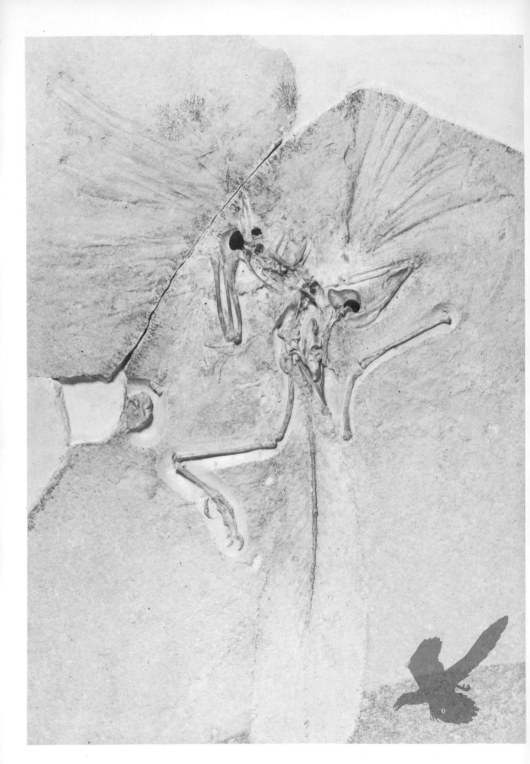

ism within the cell – and the globins, which will serve as an example here.

Globins are a family of proteins which occur in some micro-organisms and plants, and in many animals, and are concerned with oxygen transport and storage. Globin molecules contain about 150 amino acids. In plants, in most invertebrate animals and in the jawless vertebrates (lampreys and their relatives) there is usually only one type of globin in each species. In other vertebrates there are two varieties of globin – myoglobin, which acts as an oxygen store in the muscles, giving mammalian muscle and the 'dark meat' of birds its red colour; and haemoglobin, which carries oxygen in the red blood cells from the gills or lungs to the tissues. Land vertebrates have two types of haemoglobin (alpha and beta chains) and in mammals there is a third type (gamma or foetal haemoglobin) which has a greater affinity for oxygen than adult haemoglobin and allows the foetus to take up oxygen from the mother's blood. Finally, in apes and man there is a fourth type, delta chain haemoglobin, very similar to beta. Myoglobins are functional as single molecules (Fig. 9), but functional vertebrate haemoglobins consist of four chains, two alphas and two betas in most adults, two alphas and two gammas in mammalian foetuses, linked together and folded into a complicated three-dimensional shape.

In mammals, myoglobin and the three or four types of haemoglobin chain are coded by different genes which may be on different chromosomes. It is assumed that the evolutionary process responsible for the variety of higher vertebrate globins is gene duplication (Fig. 46). Originally, a single gene coded a primitive globin. By an accident of nuclear division (section 6·2) in a remote ancestor of jawed vertebrates, the portion of chromosome carrying the globin gene was duplicated. Different mutations then accumulated, by natural selection, in each copy until eventually they acquired different functions, as myoglobin and a primitive haemoglobin, probably more similar to the beta type than the alpha type, and functioning with four linked chains. Then, a second duplication of the haemoglobin gene occurred, and again the two copies accumulated different mutations, giving rise to the alpha and beta chains. In the ancestor of mammals, the beta gene duplicated again, and one copy evolved into the foetal gamma chain. Finally, in the ancestor of apes and man yet another duplication

Figure 45
The earliest true bird, *Archaeopteryx lithographica*. *Archaeopteryx* comes from Upper Jurassic rocks, about 150 million years old, in Bavaria. Five fossil skeletons have now been found, of which this one, discovered in 1861 and now in the British Museum (Natural History), was the first. *Archaeopteryx* is a bird because it has feathers, which have left impressions in the rock, and a wishbone. But it resembles dinosaurian reptiles, and differs from all living birds, in having teeth in the jaws, three clawed fingers on the wing, and a long bony tail, with many vertebrae (birds have a rudimentary tail, the 'parson's nose'). About $\frac{1}{4}$ natural size. The silhouette at bottom right suggests how *Archaeopteryx* looked in flight.

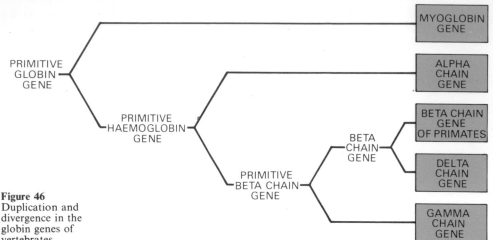

Figure 46
Duplication and
divergence in the
globin genes of
vertebrates.

and subsequent differentiation of the beta gene produced the
delta chain. This story is shown in Figure 46. The complete
history of globin genes is far more complicated than this, with
duplications in lampreys, fishes, and so on, and other equally
intricate examples are known, such as the immunoglobulin
(antibody) system of vertebrates. In man there are at least fifteen different immunoglobin genes, all the result of repeated
duplications and differentiations from a single ancestral gene
in some early jawed vertebrate.

The sequence of the amino acids in the globin molecules has
been worked out in a large number of vertebrate species, a
few invertebrates and a couple of plants. From these sequences
it is possible, by mathematical analysis, to derive a genealogical tree, in which each branch requires as few mutations as
possible, and in which the branching points and the base of
the whole tree represent hypothetical ancestral globin
sequences. This process is analogous to the method of deriving
a genealogy or *phylogeny* from series of homologous characters,
described in section 11.1. Part of the genealogy derived from
globin sequences is shown in Figure 47, with the number of
point mutations in DNA necessary to link each twig and
branch. This sort of tree is, in theory, independent of the more
traditional type of evolutionary tree, based on characters of
living species or of fossils (for example, Figs 42 and 44), since
a computer, suitably programmed, could sort out a genealogy
amongst a set of protein sequences of unknown source.

It is important to avoid the mistake of thinking that these pro-

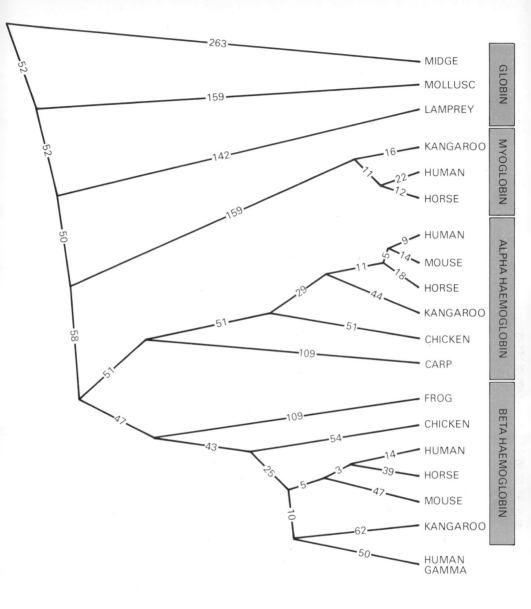

Figure 47

A genealogical tree (phylogeny) of globin molecules.

The tree was generated by computer on the basis of the sequence of amino acids in different globins. Unlike traditional evolutionary trees, diagrams of this sort may show the same species in several different places (for example, man appears four times here), because they combine information from different varieties of protein. So the branching points here include splits between genes (gene duplication, Fig. 46) as well as splits between species. The numbers on the branches of the tree are the numbers of point mutations (one-letter changes in the genetic code) needed to transform the actual or hypothetical molecule at one end of the branch into that at the other end. This tree is simplified from one containing 55 globins.

137

tein-sequence trees, because they are produced by computers and have unambiguous numbers in them, represent the actual course of evolution. They do not. The computer-generated tree is not necessarily more true or factual than one produced by a comparative anatomist who has studied the structure of a wide variety of species. The two trees will be a valuable check on one another, but each can be no better than the person who looked at the species, or wrote the computer programme. The computer can produce a great variety of trees from the same protein sequence data, depending on the kind of assumptions that are fed into it by the programmer. The comparative anatomist is certainly more fallible, because his problems are never presented to him so clearly. Usually, the two types of tree agree on most branching points, and areas of disagreement between them (as in the example in Fig. 48) are a stimulus to research and new ideas.

Looking at a smaller part of the genealogy, we can see what molecular data has to say about the relationships of the human species. The close similarity between apes and man was recognized by Linnaeus, who was the first to classify them together. But to take the next step, and infer that this similarity indicates genealogical relationship, required such boldness or disregard for sensibilities that Darwin side-stepped the issue in *The Origin of Species*; in the whole volume his only reference to the evolution of man is one cryptic sentence: 'Light will be thrown on the origin of man and his history.' Of course, it is now accepted that the apes are man's closest living relatives, and that among the four types of living ape (gibbons, orang-utans, gorillas and chimpanzees) the gorilla and chimpanzee are closest to man. Nevertheless, the difference between us and these apes seems so great that we tend to assume that the relationship is not too close.

Various molecules bearing on this relationship have been investigated. Cytochrome c, a respiratory protein, has exactly the same amino acid sequence in men and chimpanzees, and this sequence differs from that of the rhesus monkey by one mutation. Fibrinopeptides A and B (blood plasma proteins) are the same in men, chimps and gorillas, and differ from orang-utans by two mutations, and from gibbons by three or four. Human alpha and beta haemoglobin chains are the same as those of chimpanzees, while the gorilla differs in one amino acid (a single point mutation) in each chain and the gibbon

Figure 48
Two different
genealogical trees of
human populations.
A is based on
anthropologists'
measurements and
comparisons of 26
external features, such
as eye, hair and skin
colour, limb
proportions and facial
characteristics. B is
based on differences
in 58 genetic markers,
mostly blood
proteins. The two
patterns are quite
different. A cynic
might suppose that
tree A was produced
by racist
anthropologists, and
that B gives the true
history of human
differentiation. This is
not so, although tree
B is surely nearer the
truth. It is likely that
the two trees differ
mainly because the
external features used
in A are adaptations
to climate, so that the
tree recognizes
climatic groups rather
than evolutionary
groups.

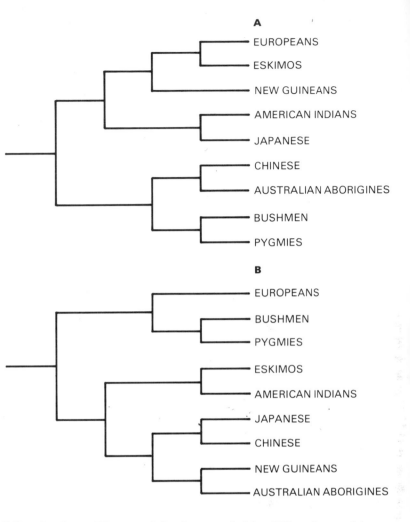

differs in three. Human delta haemoglobin differs from chimpanzee and gorilla (which are the same) in one mutation, and from gibbon in two. Human myoglobin differs from those of chimpanzee, gorilla and gibbon by one mutation (a different one in each case), and from orang-utan by two. In carbonic anhydrase, an enzyme, man and chimpanzee differ by two mutations, and man and orang-utan differ by nine. Less precise ways of comparing proteins are by serology – their reaction with antibodies – and by electrophoresis – their response to electric current. Both these methods agree in placing chimps and gorillas close to man, and orang-utans and gibbons more distant. Finally, some progress has been made in direct comparison of DNA from man and apes, by separating

139

the two chains of the double helix with heat treatment, and seeing to what extent isolated chains from one species are able to pair off with chains from another. These tests suggest chimp DNA is more like human than is gorilla, while orang-utan and gibbon are a good deal more distant. In the chromosomes, men and chimpanzees are separated by six inversions, and men and gorillas by eight (section 6.2), suggesting that we are closer to chimps, but the banding pattern of the chromosomes suggests the opposite, that we are closer to gorillas.

The meaning of these comparisons is summarized in Figure 49, showing the gradual evolution of our understanding of the relationship between men and apes. The fourth diagram (D) shows the present state of play – we cannot yet decide whether

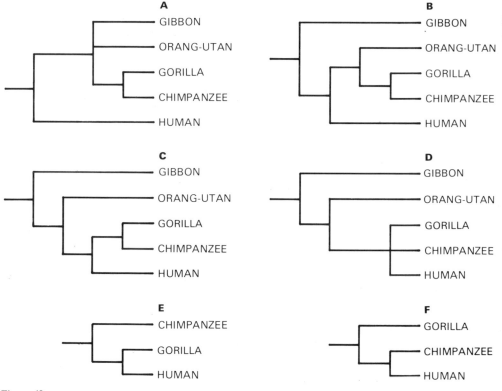

Figure 49
Different theories about how we are related to apes.
A, the traditional, pre-Darwinian view: apes form one group, and man is distinct from them. B, a scheme still found in some books, with chimps, gorillas and orang-utans as our closest relatives, and gibbons more distantly related. C, the theory found in most modern text-books, with chimps and gorillas as our closest relatives. D, the latest theory, dictated mainly by studies of proteins and chromosomes, which suggests that we cannot yet decide whether we are closest to gorillas (E) or chimps (F).

we are closest to gorillas or chimpanzees. Investigations of more proteins, or of DNA, will eventually enable us to settle on either the fifth or sixth diagrams, probably the latter. So the general conclusion from those molecules that have so far been investigated is that the genetic differences between a chimpanzee and a gorilla, slight to our eyes, are as great as those between a man and either of those animals, while the difference between an orang-utan and a chimpanzee, perhaps even slighter to us, is far greater than that between the chimp and a man. In genetic terms, we are hardly more distinct from chimpanzees than are subspecies in other groups of animals (Fig. 55). This conclusion is something of a shock to our views on the uniqueness of man, and is discussed further in section 14·1.

11·4 'Hopeful monsters'

So far in this chapter we have found that several lines of investigation, more or less independent of one another, indicate that large-scale differences, like those between man and mouse or elephant and oak tree, are produced by the same sort of causes as those which differentiate closely-related species. Men and mice or elephants and oak trees are related by common ancestry, and owe their differences to divergence, by accumulation of mutations, over enormous periods of time. The evidence for this is homology: the fact that these organisms share homologous features at many levels, the molecular (DNA, RNA, homologous proteins, etc.), the structural (cellular organization, etc.), the physiological (pathways of oxygen metabolism, etc.), in the life cycle (diploid and haploid phases, etc.), and so on.

Yet are we justified, on this evidence, in making the leap from gradual small-scale changes, like selection in peppered moths, speciation in the Galapagos, and divergence of globin molecules, to large-scale results, like the existence of elephants and oak trees? Some evolutionists have felt unhappy about this. While accepting that the gradual selection of small differences, due to point mutations and chromosome mutations, will account for the divergence within such groups as butterflies or birds, they have felt that the original appearance of birds, or land vertebrates, or vertebrates as a whole, requires innovations which cannot be satisfactorily explained by gradual, small-scale changes. So they have supposed that major innovations arise at one step, by large-scale, favourable mutations, or *macromutations*. The useful name 'hopeful monsters' is given to the original lucky carriers of such mutations. The name refers to the difference between the potential of the carrier of a typical 'monstrous' or harmful large-scale mutation, and the carrier of a true innovation. For example, we can contrast a mutation causing loss of the tail in a cat, and in the reptile-like bird *Archaeopteryx* (Fig. 45). In the first case, the result is a Manx cat, a curiosity. In the second case, the feathers on the long tail of *Archaeopteryx* might become concentrated into the fan with which modern birds control their flight.

The main reason for inventing these macromutations is that there are some features of plants and animals which can hardly be imagined as arising by gradual steps; the adaptive value of the perfected structure is easily seen, but intermediate steps seem to be useless, or even harmful. For example, what use is a lens in the eye unless it works? A distorting lens might be worse than no lens at all. What use are feathers unless they are 'proper' feathers? What use is a lung that is half-developed, and cannot give you enough oxygen? How can the segmentation of an animal like an earthworm or a centipede arise bit by bit? An animal is either segmented or it is not.

The usual answer to such questions is that they are due only to failure of imagination. Rudimentary feathers would be useful to an ancestral bird if, like living birds, it was warm-blooded, for they would help conserve heat by insulating it. Half a lung, or a quarter of a lung, would be useful to a fish, for the air-bubble would increase its buoyancy, so that it would have to expend less energy in keeping off the bottom. These two examples illustrate the principle of *preadaptation*, which explains puzzles like feathers and lungs by showing that intermediate stages in their evolution could be promoted by selection not because of their present use (flying, breathing), but for quite a different reason (heat conservation, buoyancy). We can imagine selection working on such structures for one function up to a certain threshold, beyond which a new function becomes possible, so that adaptive change is diverted into a wholly new path.

Some of the innovations requiring 'hopeful monsters' have

yielded to explanations of this sort, but others remain unsolved, and the idea of macromutations as a force in evolution persists. What form might these macromutations take? We already know one class of macromutations, doubling the entire genetic complement of an organism, in polyploidy (section 6·3). This is certainly an evolutionary force in plants, and does happen rarely in animals. Yet here the difficulty is one outlined in section 6·3. The individual in which the number of chromosomes doubles is effectively sterilized. Meiosis is seriously disturbed, and if gametes are produced, they can only meet compatible gametes by self-fertilization, or in the extremely unlikely event of meeting gametes from an individual of the opposite sex which has also suffered chromosome doubling.

Gene duplications, of the kind which produced the different globin molecules (Fig. 46) and must be responsible for many biochemical innovations, are a less conspicuous type of macromutation. Here the problems of infertility are less, for if the duplicated chromosome section is small it may hardly affect meiosis. Yet if the effects of the mutation are large, the problem of spreading the mutation is still there, for who will breed with a monster, hopeful or otherwise?

Today, speculation on macromutations mainly concerns their effects on regulatory genes, those genes that switch on and off batteries of protein-producing genes. Here, speculation is free, for we know nothing about these regulatory master genes, and that they exist is only an informed guess. The main field of operation of these genes must be embryonic development, in which cells are marshalled and differentiated to form the various organs. And we can imagine that a point mutation in a master gene controlling early development might produce changes which are small initially, when they act in the embryo, but large in the adult, through amplification in the course of development. Point mutations of this sort need not impair fertility, yet if their effects are large, the problem of the monster finding a mate remains. One possibility is interbreeding amongst the offspring of that individual which develops the mutation in its germ cells. On average, half of the offspring will carry the mutation, and through interbreeding they could establish it. In this form, the hopeful monster theory is not impossible, though orthodox evolutionists reject it. Its application to human evolution is mentioned in section 14·1.

12 Proof and disproof

The wrong view of science betrays itself in the craving to be right. Karl Popper

I have steadily endeavoured to keep my mind free, so as to give up any hypothesis, however much beloved (and I cannot resist forming one on every subject) as soon as facts are shown to be opposed to it. Charles Darwin, *Autobiography*

12·1 Science versus pseudo-science

Is the theory of evolution by natural selection proved? After so many pages of fact and argument, some may be disconcerted by a negative answer, and to read that certainty can no more be found in science than in any other way of thought. These ideas come from Sir Karl Popper, the great philosopher of science. Popper shows that proof, or certainty, exists only in mathematics and in logic, where it is trivial in the sense that the proven conclusions were already hidden in the premises. He thinks that science is distinguished from non-science (not nonsense), or metaphysics, or myth, not by proof, but by the possibility of disproof. The only characteristic of scientific theories is that they have consequences which might be falsified by observation or experiment, and a scientist is a person who is willing to relinquish his theory when it is falsified or refuted. Pseudo-scientific or metaphysical theories do not expose themselves to disproof in this way.

The classic example in science is Newton's theory of gravitation, which was the foundation of physics for more than two hundred years, and seemed to be the epitome of established knowledge, or scientific certainty. Yet in this century, Newton's theory was replaced by Einstein's, and this replacement was the consequence of observations (principally of the eclipse of the sun in 1919) which tested the two theories and disproved one of them. Of course, Newton's theory was not shown to be completely wrong; it was found to be less universal and so further from the truth than Einstein's. Nor was Einstein's theory shown to be true; it may be replaced by another, more inclusive or general theory, even closer to the truth, at any time. And we shall never know whether this process of replacement has stopped, for that would mean that we had arrived at the truth, and even if we have found it, we have no criteria for recognizing truth (sincere belief and consensus are often mistaken for such criteria).

Popper's favourite examples of pseudo-scientific or metaphysical theories are psychoanalysis and astrology. Freudian psychology, for example, predicts that neuroses and other mental disorders are the result of incidents in early childhood. But there is no conceivable observation that can clash with this theory, and any behaviour or recollected incident may seem to confirm a diagnosis of a particular patient (once a person is authoritatively diagnosed as a mental patient, any behaviour seems to fit the diagnosis). The difference between a scientist and a pseudo-scientist is, in Popper's view, that the first will look for the most severe tests of his theories, and will not take evasive action if they fail those tests, while the pseudo-scientist will look for evidence confirming his ideas and, if he feels his theory is threatened, may avoid refutation by erecting subsidiary, defensive theories around it.

12·2   Is evolution science?

If we accept Popper's distinctions between science and non-science, we must ask first whether the theory of evolution by natural selection is scientific or pseudo-scientific (metaphysical). That question covers two quite separate aspects of evolutionary theory. The first is the general thesis that evolution has occurred – all animal and plant species are related by common ancestry – and the second is the idea that the cause of evolution is natural selection (in fact, Darwin arrived at the first idea about three years before the second).

Taking the first part of the theory, that evolution has occurred, it says that the history of life is a single process of species-splitting and progression. This process must be unique and unrepeatable, like the history of England. This part of the theory is therefore a historical theory, about unique events, and unique events are, by definition, not part of science, for they are unrepeatable and so not subject to test. Historians cannot predict the future (or are deluded when they try to), and they cannot explain the past, but only interpret it. And there is no decisive way of testing their alternative interpretations. For the same reasons, evolutionary biologists can make no predictions about the future evolution of any particular species, and they cannot explain past evolution, but only produce interpretations, or stories, about it. Yet biologists have enormous advantages over historians. Firstly, they have a coherent, and scientific, theory of genetics, and their interpretations must be consistent with it. Secondly, they have one basic tool, homology (section 11·1). And thirdly, they have the universal scientific principle of parsimony, or economy of hypothesis, also known as Occam's razor: the simplest story is the best. In spite of these advantages for the evolutionist, it remains true that there are no laws of evolution comparable to the laws of physics, just as there are no laws of history.

The theory of evolution is thus neither fully scientific, like physics, for example, nor unscientific, like history. Although it has no laws, it does have rules, and it does make general predictions about the properties of organisms. It therefore lays itself open to disproof. Darwin cited several sorts of observations which would, in his view, destroy his theory. In this he was certainly more candid than his opponents. The potential tests Darwin mentioned are: 'If it could be demonstrated that any complex organ existed, which could not possibly have been formed by numerous, successive, slight modifications, my theory would absolutely break down'; 'certain naturalists believe that very many structures have been created for beauty in the eyes of man, or for mere variety. This doctrine, if true, would be absolutely fatal to my theory'; 'if it could be proved that any part of the structure of any one species had been formed for the exclusive good of another species, it would annihilate my theory'.

Darwin's potential tests may strike the reader as pretty feeble, or as tests of natural selection rather than evolution. But many discoveries, not foreseen by Darwin, provide more severe tests of the theory. These include Mendelian genetics; the real age of the earth; the universality of DNA and the genetic code; and the evidence of protein biochemistry. Evolution has survived all these with flying colours.

Turning now to the second aspect of the theory, that natural selection is the cause of evolution, many critics have held that this is not scientific because the expression 'survival of the fittest' makes no predictions except 'what survives is fit', and so is tautologous, or an empty repetition of words. For example, if we ask 'which are the fittest?' one answer might be 'those that survive', so that 'survival of the fittest' means only 'survival of the survivors'. Indeed, natural selection theory can be presented in the form of a deductive argument, for example:

1. All organisms must reproduce;
2. All organisms exhibit hereditary variations;
3. Hereditary variations differ in their effect on reproduction;
4. Therefore variations with favourable effects on reproduction will succeed, those with unfavourable effects will fail, and organisms will change.

In this sense, natural selection is not a scientific theory, but a truism, something that is proven to be true, like one of Euclid's theorems: if statements 1–3 are true, so is statement 4. This argument shows that natural selection must occur, but it does not say that natural selection is the only cause of evolution, and when natural selection is generalized as the explanation of all evolutionary change, or of every feature of every organism, it becomes so all-embracing that it is in much the same class as Freudian psychology and astrology. A final difficulty is the one explained in section 7·2, in the discussion of genetic drift. Modern evolutionary theory does not say that all evolutionary change is caused by natural selection: random effects, like genetic drift, have played a part. Natural selection is therefore protected from falsification by the alternative explanation, random effects.

12·3   Alternative theories

Using Popper's criterion, we must conclude that evolutionary theory is not testable in the same way as a theory in physics, or chemistry, or genetics, by experiments designed to falsify it. But the essence of scientific method is not testing a single theory to destruction; it is testing two (or more) rival theories, like Newton's and Einstein's, and accepting the one that passes more or stricter tests until a better theory turns up. So we must look at evolution theory and natural selection theory in terms of their performance against their competitors.

I will deal with evolution first, the belief that all organisms are related by descent and have diverged through a natural, historical process. This theory has only one main competitor, creation theory, though there are different stories of how the Creator went about His work. All creation theories are purely metaphysical. They make no predictions about the activities of the Creator, except that life as we know it is the result of His plan. Since we do not know the plan, no observation can be inconsistent with it. At one extreme there is the fundamentalist view that evidence of evolution, such as fossils, was built into the newly-created rocks to tempt us or test our faith. At the other extreme is the person to whom evidence of evolution only pushes the activity of the Creator further and further into the past. Both these modifications of the original creation myths are typical evasive moves, avoiding refutation or confrontation by modifying the original theory, or erecting subsidiary defensive theories around it.

Natural selection theory, the belief that evolution has been caused by the gradual accumulation, in different diverging lineages, of small, favourable genetic mutations, has several competitors. They include vitalist theories which accept that evolution has occurred, but propose that its course has been guided or directed towards certain ends by some vital force, universal consciousness or striving for perfection. Secondly, the idea that evolution proceeds by the inheritance of modifications acquired, through use or disuse, during the life of individual organisms, the theory first proposed (in 1809) by the French naturalist Lamarck (Fig. 57). And thirdly, a number of theories which accept evolution by natural selection on the small scale, but invoke large-scale, unique mutations as the source of major steps in evolution like the origin of the animal phyla, or of birds or flowering plants.

How does natural selection theory compare with these? Vitalist theories are purely metaphysical, for they make no predictions about the past or future activities of the various occult agents which are supposed to guide or direct evolution. Most vitalist theories seem to be only modified creation theories. Lamarckian theory, hinging on the inheritance of acquired characters (education by the environment rather than selection by it), suffered a severe reverse early in this century from the work of geneticists, who could find no good examples of the process, and no mechanism which could bring it about.

The theory seems to have been effectively disproved by the unravelling of the genetic code and the way in which it is transcribed and translated, for this is a one-way process, with no feedback through which information can be passed from the cell into the DNA.

Finally, there are the macromutation theories, discussed in section 11·4, supposing that major groups and innovations appear not by gradual selective change, but by a special class of large-scale, unique mutations. Since these theories invoke unique events in the distant past, they are not testable. They predict that 'missing links' will continue to elude us, but finding some such links will not disprove the theories, for there will still be other groups that are not linked. I know of only one attempt to test macromutation theory, a recently published demonstration that the adult size of members of species in many groups of animals does not vary gradually, but in jumps, the ratio between the size of one species and another being 1:2, or 1:4 or 1:8. In primates (men, apes and monkeys), for example, the ratios are 1:8:64:512, rising in eightfold steps. These results are consistent with macromutation, and are interesting. But they were produced by believers in macromutation, whose statistical methods have already been criticized by mathematical selectionists.

12·4   A metaphysical research programme

So, at present, we are left with neo-Darwinian theory: that evolution has occurred, and has been directed mainly by natural selection, with random contributions from genetic drift, and perhaps the occasional hopeful monster. In this form, the theory is not scientific by Popper's standards. Indeed, Popper calls the theory of evolution not a scientific theory but 'a metaphysical research programme'. He means that though the theory is closer to metaphysics than to science, accepting it as true gives us a research programme, a new way of looking at and investigating the world. And through this research programme we can make progress in understanding the world. As one criterion of progress in science, Popper offers this: 'If the progress is significant then the new problems will differ from the old problems: the new problems will be on a radically different level of depth.' It is surely true that the problems which occupy today's workers in molecular evolution are on a radically different level of depth from those which interested mid-Victorian evolutionists.

Yet Popper warns of a danger: 'A theory, even a scientific theory, may became an intellectual fashion, a substitute for religion, an entrenched dogma.' This has certainly been true of evolutionary theory, and it leads into a different view of scientific progress that has been developed mainly by the American philosopher and historian, Thomas S. Kuhn. His ideas are as much concerned with the sociology of science as with its philosophy – they deal with how science is done, not with how it might be done, as Popper's do.

In Kuhn's view, the progress of science is neither orderly nor even rational, but proceeds in lurches, with long calm periods, and occasional revolutions. In the calm periods – what Kuhn calls 'normal science' – some high-level theory is accepted by the scientific community, and research is devoted to solving puzzles within the framework provided by that theory. Observations that conflict with the theory (that seem to disprove it) are pushed to one side, or avoided by defensive sub-theories. But sooner or later, perhaps because of a build-up of these awkward observations, a crisis develops and a new high-level theory is proposed. Some scientists are 'converted' to the new theory, and begin puzzle-solving within it; others will stick with the old theory, and a dialogue between the two groups, or a decisive confrontation of the two theories, is hardly possible, for members of opposing groups interpret the world in the light of their own theory, and words will have different meanings for them. In these conflicts, the eventual success of the new theory (or the old) is not due to proof, disproof or logic, but to factors which are effective in politics, religion or art – conversion, faith, taste.

Kuhn's views, cynical as they may sound when summarized like this, certainly find echoes in the history of evolutionary theory. As a simple example of the impossibility of dialogue between supporters of opposing theories, I will cite Darwin's most powerful opponent in America, the great Swiss-born naturalist Louis Agassiz (Fig. 69). He was unmoved by *The Origin*, and remained true to the theory that species were individually created and immutable. He saw Darwin's view, that species may change and grade into one another, as a denial of the reality of species, and put to Darwin what he thought of as an unanswerable argument: 'If species do not exist, how can they vary? And if individuals alone exist, how can differences among them prove the variability of species?' To Darwin, Agassiz's unanswerable conundrum was 'an absurd logical quibble'. Both were correct, within their own framework of thought, and neither could see his opponent's point. In the same way, to Agassiz, the word 'evolution' meant the unfolding of the individual's potential, in development from the egg, and he regarded the new use of the word, by Darwin and his followers, as a gross misuse of words. Such complaints and misunderstandings are commonplace in all arguments. Here, Agassiz lost the day, and the Darwinian revolution triumphed. Following it, we can recognize a series of subsidiary revolutions: the Mendelian revolution at the beginning of this century (Chapter 4), the population genetics revolution in the 1930s (Chapter 7), the DNA revolution, in the 1950s, and perhaps the neutralist revolution (section 7·2), which began in the 1960s with the discovery of overwhelming protein polymorphism in natural populations, and is still a field of conflict. Each of these has introduced a new and deeper set of problems, and a new vocabulary.

No doubt other revolutions are in store, and whether we choose to follow Popper's or Kuhn's understanding of science, the one lesson we can learn from both these thinkers is that today's theory of evolution is unlikely to be the whole truth. Yet today's neo-Darwinian theory, with all its faults, is still the best that we have. It is a fruitful theory, a stimulus to thought and research, and we should accept it until someone thinks of a better one.

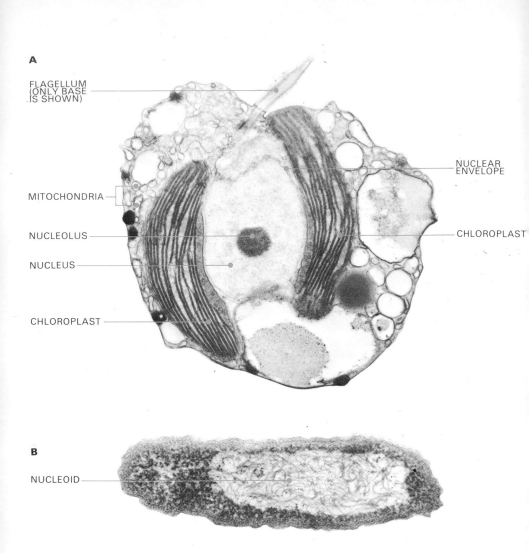

A

FLAGELLUM
(ONLY BASE
IS SHOWN)

NUCLEAR
ENVELOPE

MITOCHONDRIA

NUCLEOLUS

CHLOROPLAST

NUCLEUS

CHLOROPLAST

B

NUCLEOID

Figure 50

Eukaryote and prokaryote. Electron micrographs of sections through A, a eukaryote (a dinoflagellate, a single-celled plant) and B, a prokaryote (a bacterium). The prokaryote is very simple, with a central nucleoid not bounded by an envelope, and uniform cytoplasm. The eukaryote is much more complicated, with a discrete nucleus, and a variety of organelles and inclusions in the cytoplasm. The eukaryote is also much larger (A, enlarged $\times 14\,250$; B, $\times 69\,800$).

13
The origin and early evolution of life

Analogy would lead me one step further, namely, to the belief that all animals and plants are descended from some one proto-type.　　　　　　　　　　　　　　　　Charles Darwin

Up to this point, we have been discussing the theory of evolution in general terms. The theory leads us to believe that all present-day animals and plants are related by community of descent. The implication of that statement is that life arose once, and this book would be incomplete without a summary of ideas on how life first arose, and what were the earliest stages in evolution by natural selection. The topic is certainly intriguing, but since it concerns unique events in the remote past, it is far more speculative than is evolution theory. Rather than qualify every statement by 'it may be', or 'perhaps', I will ask the reader to remember the comments on historical explanation in section 12·2, and understand that the historical parts of this chapter are a plausible and consistent story, not fact.

Before discussing conditions in the early stages of the earth's history, we have to get some idea of the simplest and most primitive organisms alive today.

13·1　　　Prokaryotes and eukaryotes

So far in this book, I have written as if plants and animals were the only sorts of organisms. This is a simplification. Plants and animals were the only kingdoms recognized by Linnaeus, and this usage persisted until only twenty or thirty years ago. But today, with knowledge about the structure and variety of micro-organisms, from the electron microscope and from molecular biology, and with full acceptance of evolution, it is usual to recognize four or five kingdoms: Animalia, Plantae, Fungi, Protista and Monera. The scientific meaning of the first three of these names is close enough to common usage for them to be self-explanatory. Protists are single-celled organisms, or organisms which form multicellular colonies without differentiation or co-operation between the individual cells. Some, such as amoeba, are animal-like in mode of life, some are plant-like, with rigid cellulose cell walls and chlorophyll, and others fungus-like. In a four-kingdom system, each of these types can be placed with its multicellular relatives. Many protists are mobile, driving themselves along by one or more long, whip-like structures (flagella), or by many small hairs (cilia). Monerans are 'microbes', minute, single-celled organisms, usually less than one hundredth of a millimetre in diameter or length; they include bacteria, some fungus-like forms (such as streptomycetes) and some plant-like (blue-green algae).

The higher kingdoms, plants, animals, fungi and protists, are grouped together as *eukaryotes*, in contrast to the monerans, which are *prokaryotes*. This prokaryote/eukaryote distinction (Fig. 50) is one of the most profound and important in biology.

The cell nucleus, the chromosomes contained in the nucleus, the cycles of nuclear division (mitosis and meiosis) and of sexual reproduction, described in the early parts of this book, are all features of eukaryotes; none of them occurs in prokaryotes. Instead of a nucleus, prokaryotes have a 'nucleoid', an area of the cell which is not bounded by a nuclear envelope. Instead of a set of chromosomes, prokaryotes have a *chromoneme*, a double helix of DNA which is not insulated by protein like the DNA of eukaryotes, and in which the two ends are joined to form a closed loop or ring. Instead of a mitotic cycle, prokaryotes synthesize DNA continuously while active, and divide by simple fission. Instead of sexual reproduction, in which two haploid gametes unite to form a diploid zygote, those prokaryotes which have a 'sexual' process simply pass chromonemal material from one cell, the donor, to another, the recipient. Prokaryotes do not have cilia or true flagella, and those which are motile move by gliding, by wriggling the whole cell, as in spirochaete bacteria, or by means of bacterial 'flagella' – inflexible helical rods which rotate like propellors.

The other essential difference between prokaryotes and eukaryotes is that prokaryotes do not have *mitochondria* or *chloroplasts*. Virtually all eukaryote cells contain numerous mitochondria. These are minute inclusions, bounded by a membrane with internal partitions. They contain the enzyme systems responsible for oxygen metabolism, the oxidation or 'burning' of food molecules. Chloroplasts are the green, red, yellow or brown bodies found in the cells of plants. Like mitochondria, they are membrane-bounded, have internal partitions, and there are usually several to each cell. Chloroplasts contain, and synthesize, chlorophylls, and are the sites of photosynthesis, the process in which energy from sunlight is 'fixed', sugars are synthesized from carbon dioxide and water, and oxygen is given off as a waste product. In prokaryotes, which have no mitochondria, enzymes responsible for oxygen metabolism are scattered throughout the cell, or are missing altogether. Those prokaryotes which lack these enzymes live without oxygen, and most of them are killed if they come into contact with it. Photosynthesis occurs in some prokaryotes, but again the pigments and enzymes responsible for it are not packaged. And in many prokaryotes photosynthesis follows chemical pathways which do not result in oxygen production.

These differences between prokaryotes and eukaryotes are profound: they are greater than those between a man and a tree. In every feature, prokaryotes are simpler and more primitive than eukaryotes, and this suggests that in speculating about the origin of life, it is the origin of prokaryotes that we should think of, not the more complicated eukaryotes. The primacy of prokaryotes is confirmed by the fossil record. Figure 43 shows the geological time-scale and the first appearance of fossil representatives of different groups. Recognizable multicellular animals and plants do not appear until latest Precambrian times, about six to seven hundred million years ago. Protists, unicellular eukaryotic organisms, may have existed about one thousand million years ago, but the prokaryotes extend back more than three thousand million years. The earth is about 4600 million years old, so for at least 45 per cent of this enormous span of time the only fossils found are prokaryotes, resembling living bacteria and blue-green algae. The problem of the origin of life can therefore be narrowed down to the problem of how prokaryotes originated.

The relationship between prokaryotes and eukaryotes is discussed in section 13·3 – at this stage it is only necessary to say that prokaryotes and eukaryotes have so many fundamental features in common, especially the method of transmitting information in a triplet code in DNA and translating it through

155

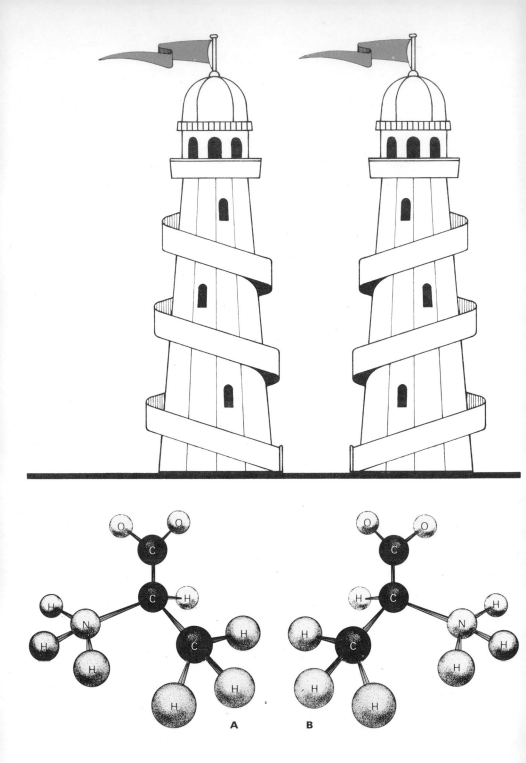

A   B

Figure 51
Dissymmetry of
biological molecules.
The two helter-
skelters, with
clockwise and anti-
clockwise spirals, are
examples of mirror-
image structures.
Below are models of
the molecule of the
amino acid alanine. A
is the 'L' (laevo-
rotatory) form, the
only one synthesized
in living organisms,
and B is the 'D'
(dextro-rotatory) form.
Atoms are labelled:
C, carbon; H,
hydrogen; N,
nitrogen; and O,
oxygen.

RNA, that the most economical theory is that eukaryotes evolved from prokaryotes, and that life as we know it originated once only, when these genetic mechanisms became established. There is one other important fact bearing on this conclusion, the 'handedness' or dissymmetry of biological molecules. Sugars, amino acids and many other chemical compounds are asymmetrical molecules, which can exist in two forms, mirror images of each other (Fig. 51). These two forms can be detected by their effect on polarized light. A solution containing equal quantities of the two forms, 'left-handed' and 'right-handed' molecules, will transmit a beam of polarized light unchanged. But a solution containing mainly or only right-handed molecules will rotate the beam in one direction, and left-handed molecules will rotate it the other way. According to their effect on the beam, the two varieties are called laevo-rotatory (to the left, abbreviated as 'L') and dextro-rotatory (to the right, 'D'). The handedness of a simple molecule does not affect its chemical properties, except in reactions with other asymmetrical molecules.

If a sugar or an amino acid is chemically synthesized in a test-tube, the product will be a mixture of left-handed and right-handed molecules, in roughly equal numbers. But in living organisms of every sort, all the amino acids are L-amino acids, and in nucleic acids all the sugars are D-molecules. It is presumably accidental that life originated with this combination, because the alternative, D-amino acids and L-sugars, should work just as well. But this uniformity in handedness is further evidence that life originated once only.

13·2   The origin of prokaryotes

We know that prokaryotes, the simplest surviving forms of life, first appeared at some time between the origin of the earth, about 4600 million years ago, and their first occurrence as fossils, about 3000 million years ago. We can only speculate about how they originated, but there are three interconnected ways of approaching the problem. First, we can try to reconstruct the conditions that existed on the earth's surface in those remote times. Second, we can simulate those conditions experimentally and see what is produced. And third, we can survey living prokaryotes and try to reconstruct their common ancestor, the simplest conceivable prokaryote.

One of the most striking things about prokaryotes is that many are anaerobic – they can only live in the absence of oxygen, which is toxic to them. Some of these anaerobic prokaryotes have various photosynthetic processes which differ from 'normal' photosynthesis, as in green plants (eukaryotes) and blue-green algae (prokaryotes), in that oxygen is not produced as a waste product. Oxygen is a reactive element, easily combined with others, and free oxygen (O_2) could hardly have existed in the atmosphere of the primitive earth. It seems certain that the free oxygen which now forms about 20 per cent of the atmosphere has been produced by past photosynthetic activity of plants and blue-green algae. The primitive atmosphere, when life first appeared, would therefore have contained no free oxygen. This means that the first organisms would have been anaerobic, but it also has another consequence. Today, the earth is surrounded by a layer of ozone (O_3; 'condensed' oxygen) in the upper atmosphere. Ozone absorbs ultraviolet light, and shields the earth's surface from this important part of the sun's energy – this is fortunate, because strong ultraviolet radiation kills all forms of life. So in the primitive atmosphere there was no oxygen and no ozone shield against ultraviolet radiation.

The composition of the primitive atmosphere is more controversial, but hints come from the constituents of volcanic gases and other sources. The primitive atmosphere probably contained hydrogen (H_2), nitrogen (N_2), some methane (CH_4), ammonia (NH_4), carbon dioxide (CO_2) and carbon monoxide (CO), and water vapour (H_2O). Liquid water was also certainly present, in the primitive oceans, because life originated in water rather than on dry land. The ocean would have contained all the atmospheric gases in solution.

With no ozone shield against ultraviolet radiation, the energy from the sun reaching the earth's surface would have been far greater than it is today, and the radioactivity of the earth's crust would also have been greater. Other sources of energy would include electric discharge (lightning, etc.), and volcanic activity. Experiments have been conducted in which gas mixtures simulating various estimates of the primitive atmosphere are subjected to ultraviolet radiation, or electric discharge, heat, shock waves and so on. The products of these experiments are surprising. A variety of organic compounds is produced, and major components are amino acids (including most of the biologically important ones), purines and pyrimidines (including the four bases in DNA – adenine, cytosine, guanine and thymine), sugars, porphyrins (molecules which are the forerunners of important biological compounds like vitamin B_{12}, chlorophylls, etc.) and complex tar-like compounds which defy analysis. All these products are found with equal quantities of L and D molecules. That such molecules do form in abiotic (lifeless) conditions is confirmed by finding the same compounds in meteorites. In the primitive oceans, these and others products would accumulate over long periods of time, producing a thin 'soup' of organic molecules, perhaps with slicks or even surface layers of oils and tars, which would shield the underlying water from ultraviolet radiation.

There is a variety of ways in which local concentrations of organic compounds might build up in this 'primitive soup'. This might happen by evaporation of lakes or ponds, by freezing (a very efficient mechanism, since water is gradually withdrawn from solution as ice), or by adsorption on the surfaces of solids such as clay particles, or on the surface film of the water.

Turning to the other side of the gap between living and non-living matter, we can survey living prokaryotes and try to construct their common ancestor, the simplest conceivable living cell. This is not easy, because prokaryotes have a variety of peculiar ways of life. The concept 'food' almost loses meaning when applied to the bizarre diets of prokaryotes: some 'feed' on sulphur, or on iron, others on simple inorganic compounds like sulphates, nitrates, carbonates, ammonia or hydrogen sulphide. (Here, 'feed' means 'carry out controlled chemical reactions and utilize the energy released'.) The most primitive types of feeding are probably simple, rather inefficient, fermentation processes, requiring only a few enzymes and using as food simple organic molecules like glucose, lactic acid or acetates. Prokaryotes which feed in this way still exist. Some living prokaryotes are also extremely small, only about one ten-thousandth of a millimetre in diameter, and only have room for about a hundred different enzymes. Nevertheless, they have, as far as we know, the complete replication and protein synthesis machinery – DNA with a triplet code, the three types of RNA, and the enzymes controlling this system. Such creatures are very close to the simplest imaginable organism. This must have DNA, messenger, ribosomal and transfer RNAs, and enzymes, all enclosed within a simple membrane.

There is a tremendous gap between this minimal organism, and an unorganized mixture of the simple molecules from which it is built up. In the 'primitive soup', we can be sure that these simple molecules (amino acids, sugars, purines, pyrimidines, etc.) were present in abundance, but how they came together, in a co-operative whole, we do not know. It is not hard to imagine amino acids linking together into protein-like chains, and some such chains could well act as catalysts, possibly catalysing production of more of the same, so that a sort of protein reproductive cycle might develop. So far, it has proved difficult to find plausible reactions which will combine purines and pyrimidines with ribose sugar and phosphates to produce nucleotides, the building blocks of nucleic acids. But once nucleotides are synthesized, they do associate in chains and form helices, with the 'correct' base-pairing (G–C and A–T). Various molecules which were probably present in the soup, such as urea and hydrogen cyanide, catalyse these reactions. So again, it is possible that simple nucleic acids, capable of self-replication, would appear in the soup. And once a self-replicating system or systems appear, mistakes in replication (mutations) will occur, and will be subject to natural selection. But it is still a very long step from replicating proteins or nucleic acids, subject to natural selection, to the unique and complex co-operative system of proteins (built up from L-amino acids) and nucleic acids (built up from D-sugars) that characterizes life as we know it. At the moment, we cannot guess how that step was taken. All we can be sure of is that abundant time was available.

Once the primeval organism appeared, whether by a unique series of chance reactions or by some inevitable process that we have not thought of, the one thing it would not have been short of is food, because to the first organisms the 'soup' would be a nutritious broth, rich in easily available, energy-rich molecules. Reproduction in this rich medium might be extremely rapid, and the soup would soon become thinner, as the food molecules which had slowly accumulated before the origin of life were used up. Then natural selection would begin in earnest, for any mutant would have a great advantage if it could synthesize from simpler, abundant molecules some essential chemical that was in short supply. Presumably, it was by successive mutational steps like this that the first metabolic pathways were built up.

In early prokaryotes, a plausible sequence would be: first, the development of simple fermentation processes; next, the ability to 'fix' carbon dioxide, producing organic compounds by reactions involving atmospheric hydrogen; followed by the ability to fix nitrogen, producing nitrates and organic nitrogen compounds; next might come the synthesis of porphyrins and related compounds which are forerunners of the photosynthetic pigments (the chlorophylls) and of cytochromes (the basis of oxygen metabolism). The photosynthesizers would come first, and would originally have been anaerobic, using carbon dioxide and hydrogen sulphide, hydrogen or ammonia, as do some living bacteria. The aerobic (oxygen-producing) photosynthesis of blue-green algae uses carbon dioxide and water, and is a more complicated process, requiring greater energy to split the water molecule. Because this sort of photosynthesis produces oxygen, no organism could evolve it unless it already had some means of dealing with oxygen. So some form of oxygen metabolism, using cytochromes, must have preceded aerobic photosynthesis. Once blue-green algae appeared, oxygen would begin to accumulate in the atmosphere. This produced a crisis, because many existing organisms would be anaerobes, unable to tolerate free oxygen. The anaerobes would be killed off or restricted to special, oxygen-free environments unless they could develop means of tolerating or (better) utilizing oxygen. Various prokaryotes tolerate oxygen in low concentrations, but others have come to use it and rely on it. Some perform simple oxidation reactions (of iron, nitrogen, sulphides, etc.) as a source of energy. Others use cytochrome and a complex enzyme pathway to 'breathe' oxygen in the same way as we do.

13·3   The origin of eukaryotes

Simple eukaryotes, resembling living unicellular algae, are first suspected in the fossil record about 1000 million years ago. At that time, prokaryotes had been in existence for about 2000 million years, and must have been diverse. Oxygen, produced by photosynthesis in blue-green algae, had been accumulating in the atmosphere for many millions of years, since 'red beds', containing oxidized iron (rust), are dated from 2000 million years ago onwards. This atmospheric oxygen would produce the ozone shield against lethal solar ultraviolet radiation.

Eukaryotes are aerobic – they require oxygen, and metabolize it by an enzyme pathway (the Krebs cycle) which includes cytochrome. These reactions take place in packets within the cell, the mitochondria, found in virtually every eukaryote cell. The most remarkable thing about mitochondria is that they have their own genetic system, distinct from the chromosomal genes in the cell nucleus. Mitochondria contain DNA and RNA, and synthesize their own enzymes. They are capable of division (reproduction), and lead a semi-autonomous life. When a eukaryote cell divides, each of the daughter cells receives mitochondria in the cytoplasm. In some eukaryotes, division of the mitochondria is synchronized with nuclear division. In others, mitochondria become aligned on the spindle in mitosis, and are segregated into two groups at the same time as the chromosomes. However, the mitochondria are not completely autonomous, for some of their functions are coded and controlled by nuclear genes. Mitochondrial DNA is very different from that of the nucleus in base-pair ratio, and is more like the DNA of prokaryotes. All these strange facts can be explained by one theory – that mitochondria were originally independent, free-living prokaryotic organisms, resembling aerobic bacteria, and their inclusion in eukaryotic cells is an example of *symbiosis*.

Symbiosis is a term for associations between two (or more) different organisms which are of benefit to both (or all) partners (symbionts). Symbiotic associations range from the casual or part-time, like birds that pick ticks off cattle, to those that are essential for the survival of the partners, like the obligatory association between termites and the wood-digesting protists that inhabit the termite gut. Perhaps the most striking example of symbiosis is the lichens, a group of 'plants', each of which is a mixed colony of a fungus and an alga, able to survive and grow in more rigorous climatic conditions than either partner could tolerate alone. There are many symbiotic relationships in which one partner lives inside the cells of the other. For example, some of the wood-digesting protists in the termite gut themselves contain symbiotic bacteria, enclosed within the cell. Many animals, unicellular and multicellular, contain symbiotic green or blue-green algae inside their cells. How the symbiotic organisms got inside the cells is often unknown, but many cells can ingest small objects (this is how amoeba feeds, and how our white blood cells deal with bacteria), and this mechanism is a plausible source of intracellular symbionts.

Returning to mitochondria, the theory is that they were originally free-living, bacterium-like aerobic organisms. In remote Precambrian times, as oxygen accumulated in the atmosphere, some simple organism, intolerant of oxygen, avoided oxygen poisoning by ingesting, but not digesting, bacteria that could deal with it more efficiently. By natural selection, this association eventually became obligatory to both partners, and was passed on to all eukaryotes – the descendants of the original partnership. This sort of story seems to have been repeated in the origin of plants. All green plant cells contain chloroplasts, packages containing chlorophyll and the enzyme systems responsible for photosynthesis. Plant chloroplasts behave in the same way as mitochondria – they contain their own DNA and RNA, are capable of reproduction, and when the plant cell divides there is a variety of mechanisms to ensure that each daughter cell receives at least one chloroplast. So chloroplasts appear to be derived from free-living prokaryotes, blue-green algae or similar forms, that were ingested as symbionts by various primitive eukaryotes – the Precambrian ancestors of green plants and other plant-like groups. The symbiotic theory of the origin of mitochondria and chloroplasts is supported by the amino acid sequences of their proteins, and the base sequences of their RNA. These sequences are not only different from those of the surrounding cytoplasm, but in mitochondria they resemble those of bacteria, and in chloroplasts those of blue-green algae.

Some of the other major differences between prokaryotes and eukaryotes (section 13·1) may also be accounted for by symbiosis: these include mitosis (the cycle of nuclear division), flagella and cilia. Cilia and flagella are mobile, hair- or whip-like structures, projecting from the surface of the cell, which either move the organism (if it is small enough, as in protists and sperm), or move fluids past the cell (as in various ciliated tracts in our lungs, sinuses, etc.). Under the electron microscope, cilia and flagella are found to have the same structure (Fig. 52). When cut across, each shows nine bundles of protein

A

B

C

tubules spaced around the margin, and two central tubules. These tubules are always constant in size, with a diameter of 1/40 000 mm. The embedded part of the cilium or flagellum ends in a basal body, a cylindrical structure again with nine peripheral bundles of tubules, but without central tubules. These basal bodies, like mitochondria and chloroplasts, are semi-autonomous. They are able to reproduce (not by dividing, but by the development of a new basal body alongside an old one), and newly-formed basal bodies can produce cilia or flagella as outgrowths. There is some evidence that basal bodies contain DNA and RNA, and synthesize their own tubule proteins.

In form, size and activity, flagella and cilia resemble mobile, thread-like prokaryotes – the spirochaete bacteria. These have similar protein tubules to cilia and flagella, but in a variety of arrangements. Various living unicellular eukaryotes have a symbiotic relationship with spirochaetes, which are attached to the surface of the cell and project from it – they were at first mistaken for flagella. So it is possible that all organisms with ciliate or flagellate cells (virtually all eukaryotes) are descended from Precambrian organisms that acquired mobility from such a symbiotic relationship with spirochaetes, and in which the relationship later became more intimate and eventually obligatory.

Figure 52
Electron micrographs of sections through cilia and a flagellum. A, cilia on the surface of a comb-jelly (ctenophore), a marine animal, × 56 700. B, one cilium at higher magnification (× 125 000) showing the nine bundles of marginal tubules and the two central tubules. C, vertical section through the base of the flagellum of a protist, showing the basal body, where the flagellum is anchored in the cell, × 44 000.

Other structures in eukaryote cells also have nine bundles of protein tubules, like cilia, flagella and their basal bodies. The most important of these are the *centrioles*, two (or more) bodies lying near or in the nucleus which are also capable of independent reproduction. The centrioles play an essential role in mitosis, because they produce the spindle to which the chromosomes become attached. The spindle is formed of protein tubules like those inside cilia and flagella, and it seems that these spindle tubules grow out from the centrioles in the same way as cilia and flagella grow out from basal bodies. The equivalence of basal bodies and centrioles is proved in sperm cells, where the tail flagellum grows out from the centriole, and in many single-celled flagellate organisms, where the basal body of the flagellum acts as a centriole in mitosis. Mitosis cannot occur in the absence of centrioles, and there are a few living eukaryotes, including amoeba, that do not have true mitosis – apparently they have never evolved it. So if flagella and cilia are descended from symbiotic spirochaetes, it seems

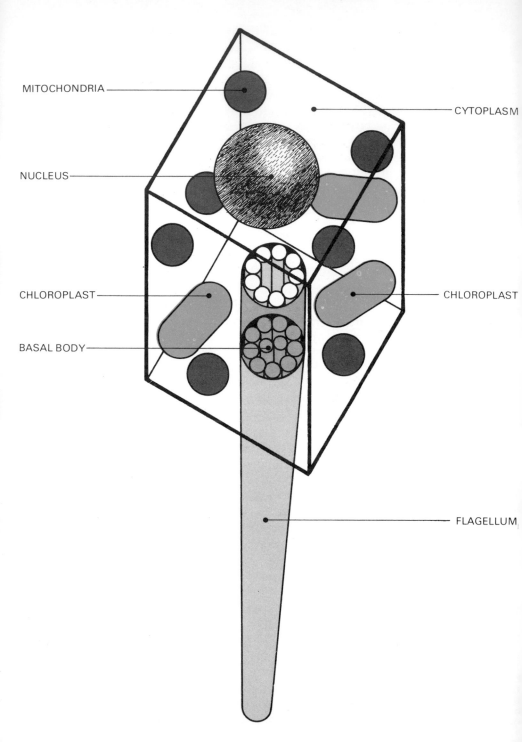

MITOCHONDRIA

CYTOPLASM

NUCLEUS

CHLOROPLAST

CHLOROPLAST

BASAL BODY

FLAGELLUM

166

that mitosis – the process in which the DNA is equally segregated into newly-formed cell nuclei – has evolved by further modification of the symbionts, now acting as centrioles and producing the mitotic spindle.

Thus a plausible story can be told about events in Precambrian times which produced the eukaryotic cell (Fig. 53). According to this story, eukaryotes are composed of three different prokaryote organisms. One, comprising the nucleus and cytoplasm, is an organism which acquired two internal symbionts. One symbiont was an aerobic bacterium, now represented by the mitochondria, the site of oxygen metabolism; the second was a spirochaete-like bacterium, now represented by cilia, flagella and centrioles. Eukaryotic plants contain a fourth symbiont, a blue-green alga, now represented by the chloroplasts – the site of photosynthesis.

13·4   The origin of sex

Mendelian genetics, as described in the early parts of this book, are only applicable to organisms that reproduce sexually, having haploid and diploid stages in the life cycle, with a reduction division (meiosis) at the transition from diploid to haploid. This complex sexual cycle does not occur in prokaryotes, and there are also a few unicellular eukaryotes that seem to lack it (some amoebae, some flagellate protists, some algae), and never to have evolved it.

Sexual reproduction must first have evolved in simple, unicellular eukaryotes. In such organisms the sexual cycle is the exact opposite of asexual reproduction: in asexual individuals the cell divides into two new ones, but in sexual reproduction two cells come together and fuse to produce a single new one. We have to ask why such an uneconomical and complicated process should evolve; what are its advantages?

One answer can be given by contrasting the history of new, advantageous mutations in sexual and asexual species (Fig. 54). Suppose that in an asexual colony of parasitic bacteria a mutation conferring resistance to streptomycin appears in one individual, and in another individual a second mutation arises, giving immunity to penicillin. Each of these mutations will be valuable, but successive treatment with the two anti-

Figure 53
The composition of a basic eukaryote plant cell, according to the symbiotic theory.

biotics will exterminate the population: it could survive only
if the two mutations were combined in one individual. This
is not possible, unless the second mutation were to arise in
a direct descendant of the bearer of the first mutation. But
in a sexual species, gametes produced by one mutant individual or its descendants can fertilize gametes produced by the
other, so combining the two mutations in one or more

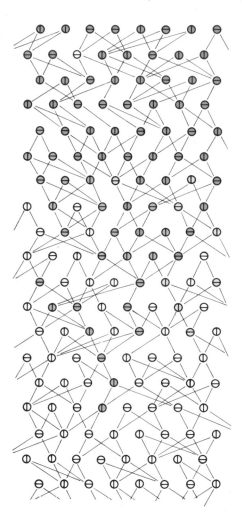
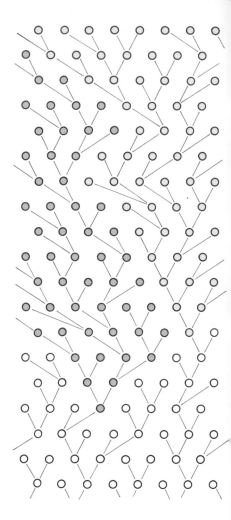

Figure 54.
The effects of natural selection in sexual and
asexual organisms. Each circle represents an
individual. In the sexual population (left) the two
sexes are indicated by a horizontal or a vertical
bar. Grey and green indicate new, advantageous

mutations. In the sexual species, two new
mutations can combine, and may spread rapidly
through the population. In the asexual species, the
two mutations are in competition, and one or
other will be eliminated.

168

members of the population. In other words, in asexual species only a single mutation, or the descendants of a single individual, can be selected at any one time, and evolution will be very slow. But in sexual species, every individual is the descendant of two members of the previous generation, and has four grandparents, eight great-grandparents, and so on, so that many different mutations can combine in one individual, and selection can act on many different mutations at the same time.

In asexual reproduction, all the descendants of one individual will be genetically identical, generation after generation, unless mutations occur. In sexual reproduction, every individual is a new, unique combination of genes, because of the reshuffling of each parent's genes in meiosis and their combination in fertilization. As a result, sexual species are much more variable, and have greater flexibility or plasticity to meet environmental changes.

So the advantages of sex are that it increases variability and the speed of evolution. The disadvantages of sex are considerable. In sexual species (except hermaphrodites) about half the population may be thought of as effectively sterile, because the next generation cannot contain more individuals than those gametes produced by one sex in the parent generation. And simply in order for sexual reproduction to occur, organisms have adopted extraordinary strategems and structures. So it is not surprising that many species, descended from sexual ancestors, have given up these stratagems and gone back to the asexual system, often by doing away with males. A population of asexual females can, in theory, produce twice as many offspring as an equal population divided into two sexes. Asexual reproduction may be by budding off new individuals, as in many plants and simple animals. Or the female may produce eggs which develop without fertilization, either by a modification of meiosis which gives diploid eggs, or after 'fertilization' of the egg by another of the haploid nuclei produced in meiosis. This sort of 'virgin birth' occurs in many insects, especially aphids (greenfly), and in many plants, including successful and familiar ones like brambles and dandelions. Greenfly and dandelions have not given up sex entirely. In greenfly, summer generations are all females, reproducing by virgin birth, but in autumn a generation of males and females is produced, and these animals mate and give rise to a new all-female generation ready for next spring. In dandelions, the western European races are triploids (p. 51), always reproduce asexually, and have given up sex entirely and irreversibly. But in central Europe there are sexual diploid races which serve as a store of variation and of new, asexual triploid races.

If a species or population gives up sex entirely, like the dandelions of western Europe, it may be very successful in the short term, and may well last for millions of years. But it will be genetically uniform, and only capable of generating variants within a narrow range. Habitats change with time, however, and such species are more likely to become extinct than their sexual competitors.

Returning to the origins of sex, the process must have first evolved in simple unicellular organisms. Today, such organisms behave rather like the greenfly mentioned above; they reproduce asexually for many generations, and mate rarely, sometimes only when conditions are deteriorating. In this way, they have the benefits of asexual reproduction (efficient increase in numbers when conditions are favourable) and of sex (increased variability). But because mating is rare in many unicellular organisms it is hard to catch them at it, and we still know far too little about the details of sexual reproduction in these simple forms. This is one of the reasons why we are still almost completely ignorant about how sex originated. The main theoretical difficulty in speculating about the evolution of sex is that natural selection works on individuals, but the only advantages of sex that we know of are not to individuals but to populations – sex increases the variability of the population. And as yet we cannot imagine how a complicated process like sex could evolve by natural selection if its only advantages are long-term ones, conferred on the population as a whole. In primitive unicellular organisms there is no differentiation of two sexes and mating involves the whole cell: two cells come together, their cell walls break down at the area of contact, the contents mingle and nuclei are exchanged. There is a resemblance here to the engulfing or eating of one cell by another, as in amoeba, and it is possible that sex, like mitochondria and chloroplasts, originated from this habit of eating other organisms. The sexual cycle is very varied in unicellular organisms. Meiosis does not always precede fertilization, as it does in plants and animals. In some protists it is the zygote, the product of fertilization, that undergoes meiosis, so that the whole life cycle is haploid except for the diploid zygote.

With the establishment of the sexual cycle in simple unicellular organisms, however it came about, the rate of evolution must have accelerated. Diverse unicellular organisms have experimented in colony formation, and from such experiments must have come different lines of multicellular organisms, represented today by fungi, plants and animals. The advantage of multicellular organization is that it allows division of labour – different cells or groups of cells can become specialized for different functions. Some become digesters, some sensors, or movers, or conductors, and the reproductive function is left to a few cells – those that give rise to gametes. The 'body' of a unicellular organism is potentially immortal, because the reproductive function is not relegated to one part of it. It is only in multicellular organisms, where reproductive potential is confined to the gametes, that there evolved the burden we all carry, the certainty of death.

14 Evolution and man

In this concluding chapter I am not concerned with the historical story of how our species evolved. Accounts of human evolution rely heavily on fossils, and the number of different stories is almost as great as the number of fossils. Instead, I will describe one current controversy between fossils and molecular biology; comment on evolution and human behaviour; and finally say something to meet the reader who has got this far and asks 'how does all this affect my life?'

14·1   Fossils versus molecules

It is therefore probable that Africa was formerly inhabited by extinct apes closely allied to the gorilla and chimpanzee; and as these two species are now man's nearest allies, it is somewhat more probable that our early progenitors lived on the African continent than elsewhere.

Charles Darwin, *The Descent of Man*, 187

The traditional approach to the problem of when and where man originated has been to search for fossils. A more rigorous approach is through theories of the kind shown in Figure 49. The problem itself, when and where did man originate, has meant different things to different people. Some have chosen to define man as a species that makes tools; or is self-aware; or uses language, or reason; or walks fully upright; or whose brain exceeds a certain size. If man is defined in any one of these ways, the question 'where and when' becomes one of where and when tool-use, or language, or upright posture, etc., arose. The least ambiguous way of posing the question is through theories of the kind shown in Figure 49: in asking where and when man originated, we are interested in the speciation event that separated us from our closest relatives. If the theory shown in Figure 49A were correct, we might guess that man arose in Africa, where chimps and gorillas live; or in south-east Asia, where gibbons and orang-utans live; or somewhere in between. And we should place the split between humans and apes far in the past, more than 25 million years ago, for early Miocene and even Oligocene fossil apes are known. But if the correct theory of our relationships is one of the alternatives shown in Figure 49E and F, as it seems to be, then the fossil hunters are right to search in Africa, for both of our closest relatives are only found there, and the two successive speciations shown in Figure 49E and F should have happened there. As for when we separated from the apes (the more recent of the two speciations), the fossils say at least 5 million years ago, when very man-like fossils (*Australopithecus*) occur in Africa. In fact, fossils strongly suggest that we separated from apes more than 15 million years ago, when an animal called *Ramapithecus* lived in India, south-east Europe, Turkey and Africa. *Ramapithecus* is known only by fragments, but features of the jaws indicate that it is related to men rather than to apes.

Here, the evidence summarized in Figure 55 is relevant. Information from a large number of proteins, and other genetic evidence, shows that the genetic distance between us and chimpanzees is little more than that between subspecies in other groups. When many different proteins are considered, as in the human/chimpanzee comparison, it is possible to use the genetic distance as a very rough (or inaccurate) evolutionary

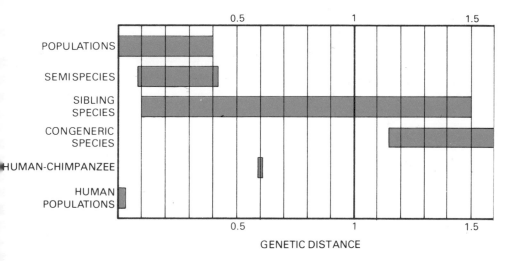

GENETIC DISTANCE

Figure 55
Genetic distance between humans, chimpanzees and other animals.
The upper part of the diagram is a large-scale version of Figure 31, where the scale is explained. The distance between humans and chimpanzees (fifth bar) falls in the range of sibling species (third bar). Humans and chimps are placed in separate genera (*Homo*, *Pan*) and families (Hominidae, Pongidae), yet they differ in less than one per cent of their genetic material, and the distance between them is absurdly low when compared with species that are placed in the same genus (fourth bar). The range in human populations (bottom bar) is also low compared with that in some other species (top).

173

clock. By comparison with protein divergence between other mammals, the distance between us and chimpanzees implies a time of divergence of perhaps 1–5 million years. This is an absurdly low figure when compared with the currently accepted estimate from fossils – 15 million years or more. What has gone wrong? There are several possibilities. One is that the fossil estimate is wrong; wishful thinking has misled the palaeontologists into seeing early fossils like *Ramapithecus* as human ancestors. A second possibility is that men and apes have evolved more slowly than other mammals: the evolutionary clock has been running down in our lineage. This could be caused by the long generation time of men and apes compared with that of the average mammal, for evolution should be paced by generations rather than years. A less likely explanation is that protein evolution has slowed down in men and apes because their biochemistry is so refined that it leaves little room for improvement. A third possibility is that the genetic markers used to estimate the human/chimpanzee difference in Figure 55 are a biased sample: the available techniques have not yet given us access to the real genetic differences. A final possibility, linked with the last two, is that the differentiation of men from chimpanzees has entailed little change in proteins, the product of 'normal' structural genes, but instead has involved changes in regulatory genes, which control the structural genes (by switching them on and off, section 4·3) and so regulate the growth and development of the organism. This is the explanation favoured by the workers who calculated the human/chimp genetic distance shown in Figure 55.

The anatomical differences between people and chimpanzees, though striking to our eyes, are not profound. And when adult humans are compared with young stages (late embryos and juveniles) of the chimpanzee and gorilla, many of the most striking differences disappear. Our large brains, bulbous skulls, flat faces and lack of hair are all found in embryo apes. The differences between us and chimpanzees could be due to a few, perhaps only one or two, mutations in the regulatory genes that control our development. As a result, human development is slowed down or retarded, and hence the helplessness and huge, lolling head of new-born babies; the late eruption of our teeth; and our very long period of infancy and growth, which allows the learning, from parents and others, that is so characteristic of mankind. The human gestation period is the same as that of gorillas, and only six weeks longer than that of chimpanzees, yet our postnatal period of immaturity, about 18 years, is twice that of these apes, as is our lifespan.

These facts, showing that human development is relatively retarded, are undisputed. But the explanation, that they are caused by a few mutations in regulatory genes, can be disputed. For this argument – large effects produced by a few mutations – is a familiar one, the theory of macromutation (section 11·4). Most evolutionists reject macromutations as an effective force in evolution, and if evolutionists can only save the uniqueness of their own species by reinstating macromutation, perhaps they are no more free of the shackles of prejudice than anyone else. But at least investigation of human evolution is turning away from the search for fossil ancestors, and towards closer comparison with our nearest non-human relatives. Attempts to educate young chimpanzees are having some success, when the animals are taught sign-language, which they can reproduce, rather than speech, which they cannot. These experiments, and others, suggest that tool-use, language, reason and self-awareness are not the uniquely human capacities we once thought them to be.

Of course, all this does not reduce the gap between ourselves and chimpanzees to nothing. For example, there is the chromosome fusion which gives us 46 chromosomes, whereas chimps and other apes have 48, and the six inversions of parts of chromosomes which differentiate us from chimpanzees (section 6·2). These chromosome differences are sufficient, I hope, to frustrate anyone who is brave (or insensitive) enough to persevere with the ultimate experiment, trying to hybridize the two species.

14·2   Sociobiology

A woman is only a woman, but a good cigar is a smoke.
                                                    Rudyard Kipling

In 1975 Professor Edward O. Wilson, of Harvard University, published a large and scholarly text-book called *Sociobiology*. Wilson is an evolutionist, ecologist and animal behaviourist who specializes in insects. In this book, he sought to establish sociobiology as a new scientific discipline, in which the theories of evolution, ecology and ethology (study of behaviour) could be combined in a coherent whole, dealing with the social life of animals (plants, and the simplest animals, have no recognizable social life). In the last chapter of a long book, after reviewing the whole animal kingdom. Wilson applied his ideas to human society, to synthesize sociology with sociobiology. This chapter has created a heated controversy, reflected in books and articles published since then.

On Wilson's side in the controversy are those who believe, like him, that we have not cast off the effects of our ancestry – our close kinship with the apes, and, more remotely, with monkeys, other mammals and other vertebrates. They believe, for example, that kin selection (section 8·5) is applicable to human societies, and that our altruism is due to 'genes for altruism', and has been shaped by the same selective forces as those which have produced sterile worker castes in social insects. They hold that the concept of 'investment ratio', discussed in section 8·5 in connection with social insects, gives a genetic basis for the male-chauvinist epigraph to this section, or for the rhyme that was the only fruit of the philosopher William James's experience with drugs:

> Higamus hogamus,
> Woman is monogamous.
> Hogamus higamus,
> Man is polygamous.

According to this interpretation, women are necessarily tied to their children, and will pass on their genes most effectively by selecting, as mates, males who will stay with them. Fidelity can be tested, for example, by the woman insisting on a long courtship. Males, on the other hand, can pass on their genes most effectively by promiscuity, for their investment in each child may be minimal. Theories of this sort can explain dowries, male dominance, and other unfashionable aspects of society.

Ranged against the sociobiologists are those who emphasize not our evolutionary heritage through kinship with other animals, but our own unique and fast-moving vehicle of change, cultural evolution. In simple animals and in plants, the only information passed from generation to generation is the information in the genes. Change can come about only by changes in the genes, and is necessarily slow. In higher animals, such as mammals, parental care of the young allows more information to be passed on: the young are capable of learning by imitating their parents. In our species, this instruction of the young has been taken much further, but in addition there is a new and highly effective means of transmitting information, through the spoken word, the written word, and all the other artefacts that we have learned to produce. Through these channels we can learn not only from our parents and social group, but from the work of people long dead, or on other continents. The pace of cultural evolution has been accelerating wildly over the last century or so, but it has plainly been an effective force since the invention of writing, and must, through oral tradition, have been acting since language first developed. Given cultural evolution, the manifest flexibility of the human brain, and the opportunities we have to analyse our own behaviour, through introspection, the 'anti-sociobiologists' contend that we have thrown off our brutish heritage, and that our behaviour is dominated not by our genes, but by reason, training, tradition, fashion and all the other forces to which we are exposed.

Which side is right? Science cannot help here, for there is, as yet, virtually no evidence to set on either side. There is no clear evidence that any trait of human behaviour is genetically determined, except for a possible correlation between criminal violence and an extra chromosome in certain males. Nor is there any clear evidence that any behavioural trait is not genetically determined, except that neither you nor I will accept that our genes have dictated the work we do, or how we will spend this evening.

The sociobiology debate is an updated version of the 'nature or nurture' controversy of the early days of genetics: do genes or the environment have the upper hand? That debate fizzled out with the answer 'partly'. In some instances, the genes win, in others, the environment, but there is no clear-cut answer (section 5·2). No doubt the same is true of genetic and cultural contributions to behaviour. The 'nature or nurture' debate was never merely scientific, but had strong political overtones. The Lamarckian doctrine, of directly inherited environmental effects, persisted in Russia until the 1960s, and, under Lysenko's leadership, dominated Soviet genetics in the 1930s and 40s. The reasons were that Lamarckian inheritance offered a shortcut to the perfectibility of man, his crops and domestic animals, that matched the Marxist programme. In the west, on the other hand, the doctrine of Darwin and Mendel, the primacy of the genes and the infinitely gradual pace of change, suited capitalist society. For example, Darwin's inheritance allowed him to devote himself to science, for it relieved him of the necessity of earning a living. His servants, too, were born to their station in life. So it is with the sociobiology debate, in my view: the left are ranged on the side of cultural evolution, rapid change and the possibility of betterment; and the right are on the side of the genes, and our heritage from the distant past.

14·3   Human nature

I see no good reason why the views given in this volume should shock the religious feelings of any one.
Charles Darwin, *The Origin of Species*

This concluding section is to meet the reader who has got this far and asks 'how does all this affect my life?' Evolution theory has been called 'what ultimately may prove to be the greatest revolution in the history of thought'. It has changed, and is changing our view of our history, purpose and future. Thousands of pages have been written on these lines, and I have no capacity to add much to them. Evolution theory in the crude form of survival of the fittest, or 'social Darwinism' as it was politely called, has been used to justify Hitler's racial policies, grinding the faces of the poor, and many other examples of man's inhumanity to man. Has it anything more positive to offer? Some people find it profoundly depressing. They read genetic and evolution theories as proof that we are the products of blind chance, nothing but pointless experiments in protein chemistry. My reply is that I find it no more depressing to be a chemical experiment than an experiment in ethics, which is the Christian message read from the same nihilist or 'nothing but' viewpoint.

It is true that evolution theory is no substitute for religion, though some have tried to make it one. But it does contain a message about our relationship to the rest of nature that is more positive than the Old Testament message: that man is unique, made in the image of God, and that the rest of creation is there for him to exploit. It will take us a long time completely to lose this attitude, although its results are daily more obtrusive. The message of evolution is that we are not unique. We are animals, members of the same lineage as the woodlouse and the shrew. We are social mammals, and as such our purpose is not merely to reproduce, yet our racial pride or patriotism and our social striving may be no more or less commendable than the tribal loyalty of baboons. Our uniqueness lies in our brains, tongues and hands, that have allowed us to accumulate knowledge (or to decrease ignorance), building on the experience of previous generations in a way that no other species can. It is consciousness of the past and anticipation of the future, derived from this knowledge, that give us control over the beasts of the field. And if we are alone in the universe, we are alone in the sense that we are our own masters, and have no one to blame but ourselves, for if the future is anywhere it it is in our heads.

15 Who's Who

Before Darwin

Figure 56
Carl Linnaeus (1707–1778), the Swedish naturalist, professor of botany at Uppsala, who laid the foundation of systematic biology with his method of naming and classifying animals and plants (see p. 121). Modern botanical nomenclature dates from 1753 (Linnaeus's *Species Plantarum*), and zoological nomenclature from 1758 (Linnaeus's *Systema Naturae*, 10th edition). Linnaeus was no evolutionist, but his system of classification is readily adapted to evolutionary interpretation (Fig. 41). This lithograph is from a portrait of Linnaeus in old age (1775). Courtesy of the Linnean Society.

Figure 57
Lamarck (Jean-Baptiste-Pierre-Antoine de Monet, chevalier de Lamarck, 1744–1829), the French naturalist who was the first man to publish a reasoned theory of evolution (or transformism, as it was then called), in his *Philosophie Zoologique* (1809). Lamarck is unfortunate to be remembered today chiefly in connection with the inheritance of acquired characters (p. 148). In France, he is regarded as the father of evolution, yet he died in poverty and was vilified by the scientific establishment of his time, especially by Baron Cuvier, the greatest authority in zoology and a believer in the theory that the history of life consists of repeated creations and catastrophic extinctions. Darwin, too, was unnecessarily contemptuous of Lamarck, for he also upheld the inheritance of acquired characters. This engraving shows Lamarck in 1821. Courtesy of the Linnean Society.

Figure 58
Robert Chambers (1802–1871), the Scottish writer, publisher (with his brother he founded the firm of W. & R. Chambers) and amateur geologist. In 1844 the first book on evolution in English, *Vestiges of the Natural History of Creation*, was published anonymously in London. In 1884, after his death and 40 years of rumour, Chambers was acknowledged as the author of this book. Though denounced and condemned alike by scientific and religious authorities, Chambers's book went through ten editions in ten years, and Darwin later acknowledged that it had helped to clear the ground for his own work. Chambers's thoughts may have been turned towards hereditary change (evolution) by the fact that he and his brother were born with six digits on both hands and feet. The extra fingers and toes were removed in childhood, but the operation left Robert lame. This engraving shows him aged about 60.

Darwin

Figure 59

Figure 60

Charles Robert Darwin (1809–1882), after training for medicine and the church, educated himself in science as naturalist on the surveying voyage of HMS *Beagle* (1831–1836). He began a notebook on transmutation of species in 1837, shortly after returning to England, and in 1838 hit on the idea of natural selection as an explanation of evolutionary change. With a prosperous background (his father was a successful doctor, and both his mother and his wife were Wedgwoods), Darwin worked as an amateur at his home, Down House, near Bromley, Kent. Although limited by chronic ill-health to three or four hours' work a day, he laboured for twenty years compiling material for a huge manuscript on evolution by natural selection. This work might never have gone to the printer in his lifetime, but in 1858 he received a manuscript from A. R. Wallace (Fig. 62), then in the Molluccas, which showed that Wallace had independently arrived at exactly the same theory as Darwin. Darwin and Wallace published a short joint paper in 1858, and

Darwin immediately set to work abstracting his large manuscript. The result was *The Origin of Species* (1859). Darwin published eight more books during his lifetime, the most important of which are *The Variation of Animals and Plants under Domestication* (1868), *The Descent of Man, and Selection in Relation to Sex* (1871) and *The Expression of the Emotions in Man and Animals* (1872). I recommend his autobiography, written for his children, and only published posthumously. Darwin's home, Down House, now belongs to the Royal College of Surgeons, and is open to the public as a museum of Darwiniana. Figure 59 shows Darwin in about 1857, just before he began *The Origin* (courtesy of the Linnean Society), and Figure 60 shows him in 1881, on the verandah of Down House in 'his usual out-of-doors dress'.

Darwin's friends and supporters

Figure 61
Thomas Henry Huxley (1825–1895), zoologist and educator. After qualifying as a doctor, Huxley's career was moulded, like Darwin's, during a Royal Navy surveying voyage, on HMS *Rattlesnake* (1846–1850). He was professor at the Royal School of Mines in London, and later at the Royal College of Surgeons. When *The Origin of Species* was published, Huxley was an immediate convert to Darwin's views ('How extremely stupid not to have thought of that,' he said), and he became Darwin's chief supporter in England, notably at the 1860 meeting of the British Association in Oxford, when he crossed swords with the Bishop of Oxford, and in several battles with Richard Owen (Fig. 67). A brilliant talker, writer and thinker, some of Huxley's mental qualities come across in this photograph, taken in 1857. Courtesy of the Linnean Society.

Figure 62
Alfred Russell Wallace (1823–1913), traveller and naturalist. Wallace travelled and collected on the Amazon (1848–1852) and in the Indo-Australian archipelago (1854–1862), where he independently came to the same theory as Darwin, and spurred Darwin into writing *The Origin*. In later years, Wallace published a major work on the distribution of animals, and books on travel, natural selection and evolution. He was never convinced that evolution could explain the human brain, and was an ardent socialist, spiritualist, and opponent of vaccination – something of a crank. He was also a modest and kindly man, as this 1895 photograph suggests. Courtesy of the Linnean Society.

182

Figure 63
Rev. John Stevens Henslow
(1796–1861), professor of
botany at Cambridge 1827–
1861. When Darwin was an
undergraduate at Cambridge,
reading for the church, Henslow
befriended him and was
responsible for his appointment
to the *Beagle*. He was a lifelong
correspondent with Darwin, and
was chairman of the 1860
British Association meeting at
which T. H. Huxley took up the
cudgels on Darwin's behalf. The
photograph was taken in about
1856. Courtesy of the Linnean
Society.

Figure 64
Sir Charles Lyell (1797–1875),
geologist. His book *Principles of
Geology* (1830–33) supported
uniformitarianism. the doctrine
that the distant past is to be
explained only by the forces
that we see in operation today.
These ideas were directly
opposed to the catastrophism of
Cuvier and others, and were an
inspiration to Darwin's thinking
during the voyage of the *Beagle*.
Lyell became a close friend of
Darwin, and it was to him that
Darwin appealed for advice
when he received Wallace's
manuscript in 1858. The
photograph shows him in about
1856. Courtesy of the Linnean
Society.

Figure 66
Asa Gray (1810–1888),
American botanist, professor of
botany at Harvard 1842–1888.
Gray was Darwin's chief
supporter in America. Although
he met Darwin in London in
1839 and again in 1850, the two
did not begin to correspond
until 1855 (the photograph
shows Gray at about this time).
An 1857 letter from Darwin to
Gray, summarizing Darwin's
theory, formed part of the 1858
Darwin/Wallace paper. In the
years following publication of
The Origin, Gray devoted
himself to propagating Darwin's
ideas in America, and
overcoming the influence of his
Harvard colleague Agassiz (Fig.
69). Courtesy of the Linnean
Society.

Figure 65
Sir Joseph Dalton Hooker
(1817–1911), botanist. Hooker's
father, Sir William, also a
botanist, was the first Director
of Kew Gardens. Joseph, like
Darwin and Huxley, began his
scientific career on a Royal
Navy ship, HMS *Erebus*, which
cruised the Southern Ocean
in 1839–1843. Hooker
founded the science of plant
geography, and was the first
person to whom Darwin
showed the outline of his theory
(1844). With Lyell, Hooker
arranged publication of the
Darwin/Wallace paper in 1858.
Hooker was married to
Henslow's (Fig. 63) daughter,
and succeeded his father as
Director of Kew Gardens in
1865. He is photographed in the
same year as Lyell.
Courtesy of the Linnean Society.

Darwin's opponents

Figure 67

Sir Richard Owen (1804–1892),
comparative anatomist. Owen
belongs to an entirely different
tradition from Darwin. He had
studied in Paris under Cuvier,
and was influenced by the ideals
of the German nature-
philosophers (his concepts of
homology and archetype, shown
in Fig. 40, derive from the
German school). When *The
Origin* was published, he wrote
a scathing anonymous review,
but in his scientific work he
wrote of evolution in obscure
passages that manage to suggest
both disagreement with Darwin,
and that he had thought of it
first. From 1856–1883 he was at
the British Museum as
Superintendent of Natural
History, and at the age of 75
was responsible for moving the
collections into the new building
at South Kensington, which
opened in 1881. Figure 68
shows him in about 1855, his
hand resting on the crocodile
skull shown in Fig. 40A; Figure
67 shows him in old age, about
1885. Courtesy of the Linnean
Society.

Figure 68

Figure 69
Louis Agassiz (1807–1873),
zoologist and teacher. Agassiz
was born in Switzerland and
studied in Germany, with the
nature-philosophers. Like
Owen, he was a protégé of
Cuvier, and to the end of his
life maintained Cuvier's views
on repeated creations of species
and catastrophic extinctions.
After a brilliant career in
Europe (amongst his
achievements was recognition of
the Ice Age) he went to
America in 1846, and in 1848
became professor at Harvard,
where he founded the Museum
of Comparative Zoology.
Agassiz gained a towering
reputation in America, by his
lecture tours, writing and
magnetic personality. He
opposed Darwin's theory with
all his powers, right up to his
death. The photograph shows
him at Harvard in about 1860.

Geneticists

Figure 70
Johann Gregor Mendel (1822–1884). Mendel was born in Austria, of peasant stock, and entered the Augustinian monastery at Brno in 1843. The monastery was a centre of learning and research, and Mendel was instructed in agriculture and botany, and sent to Vienna University. He was teaching at the Technical School in Brno during the period (1856–1864) when he carried out his experiments with peas (p. 15) in the monastery garden. In 1868 he became Abbot of the monastery. He continued work on hybridization of plants and of bees, but did not publish his results. He died unrecognized, and only achieved immortality in this world in 1900, when his work on peas was rediscovered, and his theory confirmed. The engraving shows him in about 1860.

Figure 71
James Watson (left) and Francis Crick in 1953, with their original model of the DNA molecule in the Cavendish Laboratory, Cambridge. Both are still active in molecular genetics. Crick (born 1916) remained at the Medical Research Council's molecular biology laboratory in Cambridge until 1977, when he moved to the Salk Institute in San Diego, California. Watson (born 1928) has been professor of biology at Harvard since 1961. Watson and Crick shared the 1962 Nobel Prize for medicine. Photo A. C. Barrington Brown and Weidenfeld & Nicolson Archives.

Further reading

General works

There are hundreds of books and many thousands of scientific papers on evolution. Most of these are written for specialists, and assume a wide background knowledge of biology. All that is provided here is a way in to that literature, for everything cited here contains a bibliography. Like all scientific fields, evolution theory is constantly changing, and this week's idea may be proved wrong next week. So the hardest thing is to keep up to date. The monthly journals *Scientific American* and *Natural History* (the latter published by the American Museum of Natural History) are available in most libraries. *Scientific American* contains three or four articles a year on the latest ideas in evolution, written for the non-specialist and with illustrations of very high calibre. *Natural History* contains a monthly column, 'This View of Life' by Stephen J. Gould, which reviews developments in evolution theory in brilliant style. A collection of Gould's essays was published in 1977 as *Ever Since Darwin*, W. W. Norton, New York.

The Life Game, Nigel Calder, BBC Publications, 1973. A lavishly illustrated book, covering much the same ground as this one, in a more vivid style but in less depth.

Evolution Explained, Peter Hutchinson, David & Charles, 1974. Very easy reading and good, clear, diagrams. Try it if this book is too hard for you.

The Theory of Evolution, John Maynard Smith, Penguin Books. First edition, 1958; second edition, 1963; third edition, 1975. Maynard Smith is a leading theorist, and his book is written at semi-popular level.

The Origin of Species, Charles Darwin. First edition, 1859, now valuable, and many later editions; one in Penguin is easily available. Well worth reading or dipping into, for it is still full of interest. It was written for the general reader, and though Darwin was not proud of his prose or his mind, both come over strongly.

Introduction to the Study of Man, J. Z. Young, Oxford University Press, in hardback and paperback, 1972. A monumental book, covering a very wide field, but with chapters on evolution.

Genetics, Evolution and Man, W. F. Bodmer and L. L. Cavalli-Sforza. W. H. Freeman, San Francisco, 1976. A text-book, concentrating on human genetics.

Evolution, T. Dobzhansky, F. J. Ayala, G. L. Stebbins and J. W. Valentine. W. H. Freeman, San Francisco, 1977. A text-book written in collaboration by four specialists. They write 'perhaps this is the last time that a reasonably comprehensive account of the theory of evolution can be encompassed in a single volume'. This opinion is contradicted by the next book.

The Science of Evolution, W. D. Stansfield. Macmillan, New York, 1977. An encyclopaedic book.

Books on particular topics

(The numbers in brackets are the chapters or sections of this book concerned with these topics.)

The Double Helix, James D. Watson, 1968. Available in Penguin; the inside story of the discovery of the structure of DNA. (4·3)

The Genetic Basis of Evolutionary Change, R. C. Lewontin. Columbia University Press, in hardback and paperback, 1974. Modern population genetics, not easy reading but a masterly book. (5, 7, 9)

Genetic Diversity and Natural Selection, J. Murray, Oliver & Boyd, in hardback and paperback, 1972. (5, 7)

Inheritance and Natural History, R. J. Berry. Collins, 1977. A 'New Naturalist' on genetics and natural selection. (5–8)

The Selfish Gene, Richard Dawkins. Oxford University Press, 1976. Evolution and genetics applied to behaviour, for the general reader. (8·5 14·2)

Darwin's Islands. A Natural History of the Galapagos, Ian Thornton. Natural History Press, New York, 1971. (10)

Molecular Evolution, F. J. Ayala (editor). Sinauer Associates, Sunderland, Mass., 1976. A collection of essays, by specialists, on different aspects of molecular evolution: fairly technical. (11·3)

Popper, Bryan Magee. Fontana Modern Masters (paperback), 1972. Easy introduction to the philosophy of science. (12)

Unended Quest, Karl Popper. Fontana (paperback), 1976. Popper's intellectual autobiography. (12)

The Structure of Scientific Revolutions, Thomas S. Kuhn. University of Chicago Press, First edition 1962; second edition 1970. (12)

The Origin of Life on the Earth, S. L. Miller and L. E. Orgel. Prentice-Hall, in hardback and paperback, 1974. (13)

Origin of Eukaryote Cells, Lynn Margulis. Yale University Press, 1970. An account of the origin of life and the symbiont theory of eukaryote origins. (13)

Chance and Necessity, Jacques Monod. Collins, in hardback and paperback, 1972. The philosophy of a molecular biologist. (14)

Natural History Museum handbooks

History of the Primates: an Introduction to the Study of Fossil Man. W. E. Le Gros Clark, 1970.

The Neolithic Revolution. Sonia Cole, 1970.

Man the Toolmaker. K. P. Oakley, 1972.

The History of Mammals. W. R. Hamilton, 1972.

Dinosaurs. W. E. Swinton, 1974.

Fossil Amphibians and Reptiles. W. E. Swinton, 1973.

Human Biology – an exhibition of ourselves. 1977.

A New Look at the Dinosaurs. A. Charig, 1978.

Glossary

Abbreviations: adj., adjective; Gr., Greek; L., Latin; n., noun; v., verb.

Words in *italics* are defined elsewhere in the glossary.

Adaptation, n., adaptive, adj. (L. *adaptare*, to fit to). A characteristic of an *organism* which fits it for a particular environment; the process in which an organism is modified towards greater fitness for its environment.

Adaptive radiation. Evolutionary divergence of a group of related *species* into different environments or ways of life.

Aerobic, adj. (Gr. *aer*, air; *bios*, life). Requiring free oxygen to live.

Allele, n. (Gr. *allelon*, one another). Any of the alternative states of a *gene*. Alleles occupy the same relative position on the *chromosome*, can mutate to one another, and pair in *meiosis*.

Amino acid, n. One of a large group of organic compounds in which the *molecule* contains an amino group (NH_2) and a carboxyl group ($COOH$); a subunit of a *protein molecule*.

Anaerobic, adj. Not requiring free oxygen to live.

Archetype, n. (Gr. model). A basic plan or general structure common to a group of *species*; a hypothetical ancestral type.

Asexual reproduction. Reproduction without sex, involving only one parent.

Bacterium (plural bacteria), n. (Gr. *bakterion*, a little rod). A member of an extensive group of minute, unicellular *prokaryote organisms*. They lack chlorophyll, and many live as parasites.

Base, n. In chemistry, substances which neutralize acids (the precise meaning is more extensive, but too intricate to explain simply).

Base-pair, n. A term used for the cross-links or 'treads' in the double spiral of the *DNA* molecule, formed by an adenine–thymine bond or a guanine–cytosine bond. A base-pair is the 'atom' of heredity.

Biological species. A term for *species* viewed as interbreeding communities, isolated from other such communities by barriers which prevent *gene flow*.

Centriole, n. A small body, found in or near the *nucleus* of each cell, which produces the spindle in nuclear division.

Chloroplast, n. (Gr. *chloros*, green; *plastos*, shaped). Self-duplicating bodies found in the *cytoplasm* of plant cells. They contain chlorophyll, and are the site of *photosynthesis*.

Chromatid, n. (Gr. *chroma*, colour; *idion*, peculiar). One of the two filaments comprising a *chromosome* during nuclear division.

Chromoneme, n. (Gr. *nema*, thread). The single loop of DNA found in *prokaryote organisms*; equivalent to the *chromosomes* of *eukaryotes*.

Chromosome, n. (Gr. *soma*, body). Thread-like bodies, comprising *DNA* and *protein*. There are several in the *nucleus* of every cell in animals and plants.

Cilia (singular cilium), n. (L. eyelash). Fur-like mobile filaments on the surface of cells.

Continental drift. The theory that the continents are not fixed but are in motion relative to each other, drifting, colliding or splitting over long periods of time (see also Tectonics).

Crossing-over, n. The process in the reduction division (*meiosis*) of reproductive cells in which pairs of *homologous chromosomes* exchange parts.

Cytochrome, n. (Gr. *cytos*, cell; *chroma*, colour). One of a group of iron-containing *enzymes*, found in most animal and plant cells, which play an essential part in oxygen respiration.

Cytoplasm, n. (Gr. *plasma*, shape, body). The living contents of a cell, except for the *nucleus*.

Deletion mutation. Loss of part of a *chromosome*.

DNA, Deoxyribose nucleic acid. A substance present in every cell (within the *nucleus* in *eukaryotes*) which gives the hereditary characteristics. See section 4·3 for its structure.

Diploid, adj. (Gr. *diplos*, double). Having two sets of *homologous chromosomes* in the *nucleus*; having double the number of *chromosomes* present in the sperm or egg-cells of the *species*.

Dominance, n., dominant, adj. A *gene* or character which is manifested when present in only one *chromosome* of a pair (a single dose, inherited from one parent only). Opposite to *recessive*.

Duplication mutation. Doubling or repetition of part of a *chromosome*.

Ecology, n., **ecological,** adj. (Gr. *oikos*, house; *logos*, reason, speech). The branch of biology dealing with the interactions between *organisms* and their environments.

Enzyme, n. (Gr. *en*, in; *zyme*, leaven). Biological catalysts; a class of *proteins* produced by organisms, which speed up chemical reactions.

Eukaryote (also spelt eucaryote), n. (Gr. *eu*, true; *karyon*, kernel). A member of the animal, plant, fungus or *protist* kingdom; an *organism* having *nuclei* and *chromosomes* in its cells. Other organisms are *prokaryotes*.

Fitness, n. Biological success or ability to cope (see p. 57 for a technical definition).

Flagellum (plural flagella), n. (L. a little whip). A whip-like, mobile filament on the surface of a cell.

Frequency, n. Abundance, commonness, number of occurrences.

Frequency-dependent selection. Increased *fitness* of a *genotype* due to its rarity.

Gamete, n. (Gr. wife, husband). A sex cell or germ cell, carrying a *haploid* set of *chromosomes*, whose function is to fuse with another gamete to produce a new individual.

Gene, n. (Gr. *genos*, race). The unit of heredity; a small piece of a *chromosome* which has a specific effect on the development of the *organism* carrying it.

Gene flow. Flow of *genes* through and between populations, over successive generations, caused by mating and migration.

Gene frequency. An estimate of the abundance of a particular *gene* in a population.

Gene-pool, n. The total variety of *genes* and *alleles* present in a *species*: interbreeding may produce any combination of these.

Genetics, n. The study of heredity.

Genetic drift. Evolutionary change in small populations produced by random effects, not by *natural selection*.

Genotype, n. The genetic constitution of an individual; all these *genes* are available for transmission to the offspring of that individual, but not all are manifested in its *phenotype*.

Genus, n. (plural genera), **generic,** adj. (L. birth). A category bearing a name such as **Homo** or **Rhododendron,** and containing one or more *species* which are each other's closest relatives. One or more genera are included in a family.

Haemoglobin, n. (Gr. *haima*, blood; L. *globus*, a ball). A red pigment, a *protein* containing iron, which readily combines with oxygen and carries it to the tissues. Found in the blood of many animals.

Haplo-diploidy. The genetic system found in ants, bees, wasps and some other insects, where males are *haploid* and females *diploid*.

Haploid, adj. (Gr. *haplos*, single). Having a single set of *chromosomes*, half the *diploid* number; the chromosome complement of *gametes*.

Hermaphrodite, n. & adj. (Gr. mythology). Having both male and female sex organs, as in many flowers and lower animals.

Heterozygote, n., **heterozygous,** adj. (Gr. *heteros*, other; *zygon*, yoke). An organism which will not breed true for a particular character, having received different *alleles* of a *gene* from each of its parents; cf. *homozygote*.

Homology, n. (Gr. *homologos*, agreement). Similarity due to common ancestry; homologous features or homologues agree in relative position and fundamental structure, but may differ in form and function.

Homologous chromosomes. A pair of *chromosomes*, one received from each parent, which have the same series of *genes*.

Homozygote, n., **homozygous,** adj. (Gr. *homos*, same). An *organism* which breeds true for a particular character, having identical *genes* in a given portion of a pair of *homologous chromosomes*.

Incomplete dominance. The situation where the *heterozygote* for two *alleles* is intermediate between the two *homozygotes*; the condition arises when both alleles are manifested in the *phenotype*.

Insertion mutation. A form of *point mutation* in which one or more extra *base-pairs* are inserted into a portion of *DNA*.

Inversion mutation. Reversal of part of a *chromosome*, so that the *genes* of that part are in inverse order.

Invertebrate, n. A multicellular animal without a backbone.

Kin selection. Selection of traits that increase the *fitness* of the family rather than the individual.

Linkage group. A number of *genes* or characters which are usually inherited together, because they are on the same *chromosome*.

Macromutation, n. (Gr. *makros*, great). A pronounced genetic change, producing an *organism* which is very different from its parents.

Meiosis, n, **meiotic,** adj. (Gr. diminution). The form of nuclear division in which the number of *chromosomes* is halved. Meiosis occurs in *gamete* formation, when a *diploid* cell produces four *haploid* gametes. The diploid number is restored when two gametes (egg, sperm) fuse.

Melanism, n., **melanic,** adj. (Gr. *melanos*, black). Darkening or blackening of an *organism* by accumulation of black pigment (melanin).

Messenger RNA. A form of *RNA* which is synthesized in the *nucleus*, each *molecule* carrying the message of one *gene*, and is translated in the *cytoplasm*, in a *ribosome*.

Metabolism, n., **metabolic,** adj. (Gr. *metabole*, change). The chemical processes through which an *organism* uses food or energy.

Mitochondrion (plural mitochondria), n. (Gr. *mitos*, thread; *chondros*, granule). Minute bodies present in *eukaryote* cells; they are self-replicating and contain *enzymes* which metabolize oxygen.

Mitosis, n., **mitotic,** adj. (Gr. *mitos*, thread). The process of nuclear division in *eukaryote* cells.

Molecular genetics. Study of heredity at the molecular level, in chemical rather than biological terms.

Molecule, n. (diminutive of L. *moles*, mass). The smallest particle of a chemical substance which can exist separately; molecules are composed of atoms.

Monera, n., **moneran,** adj. (Gr. *moneres*, single). The kingdom containing *prokaryote* organisms, such as bacteria and blue-green algae, which have no *nucleus* or *chromosomes*.

Mutant, n. & adj., **mutation,** n. (L. *mutare*, to change). A *gene* or *organism* which has undergone a heritable change. Point mutations are molecular changes within a gene; chromosome mutations are rearrangements of *chromosomes*.

Mutation rate. The average *frequency* with which a particular mutation turns up in a population.

Natural selection. The term proposed by Darwin for 'the struggle for existence' or 'the survival of the fittest'; differential mortality and reproductive success.

Nucleic acids. Complex *organic* compounds found in all cells, *DNA* in the *chromoneme* or *chromosome*, and *RNA* in the *nucleus* and *cytoplasm*.

Nucleus (plural nuclei), n. (L. a small nut). A more or less spherical body found in *eukaryote* cells: it stains deeply with dyes, and contains the *chromosomes*.

Organic, adj. In chemistry, compounds containing carbon.

Organism, n. (L. *organum*, an engine). A living individual.

Phenotype, n. (Gr. *phainein*, to appear). The appearance or characteristics of an *organism* (usually with respect to a particular feature or group of features), the result of interaction between the *genotype* and environment.

Photosynthesis, n. (Gr. *photos*, light). The characteristic process of plant life, in which energy from light is used to produce sugars; chlorophyll is the catalyst in these reactions.

Phylogeny, n., **phylogenetic,** adj. (Gr. *phylon*, race; *genesis*, origin). Study of the evolutionary history and relationships of *species*.

Phylum (plural phyla), n. The largest divisions of the plant and animal kingdoms (e.g. Mollusca, Vertebrata).

Plate tectonics. See tectonics.

Point mutation. See mutant.

Polymorphism, n., **polymorphic,** adj. (Gr. *polys*, many; *morphe*, form). The occurrence of two or more genetically distinct forms of a *species* in the same place.

Polyploid, n. & adj., **polyploidy,** n. (Gr. *polys*, many). An *organism* or *species* with three or more *haploid* sets of *chromosomes* in each *nucleus*. Triploids have three sets, tetraploids four, hexaploids six, and so on.

Population genetics. The study of heredity in populations rather than individuals – it is conducted by extrapolating from experiments on individuals, and so is largely theoretical and mathematical.

Preadaptation. The theory that complicated features may have evolved through stages in which they were adapted to quite different functions from those they now have.

Prokaryote (also spelt procaryote), n. (Gr. *pro*, before; *karyon*, kernel). A simple micro-organism which has no *nucleus*, such as a *bacterium* or blue-green alga. Equivalent to *Monera*; cf. *eukaryote*.

Protein, n. (Gr. *proteios*, primary). A group of organic compounds characteristic of living *organisms*; they are chain-like *molecules* built up from *amino acids*.

Protista (plural protists), n. (Gr. *protistos*, first of all). The kingdom of unicellular *eukaryote* organisms, including plant- and animal-like forms.

Quantum speciation. The theory that some *species* originate in a few generations, by rapid rather than gradual change.

Recessive, adj. The quality of a *gene* or character which is only manifested when present in both *chromosomes* of a pair (a double dose, inherited from both parents). Opposite of *dominant*.

RNA, Ribonucleic acid. Substance present in all *organisms* in three forms, *messenger RNA*, *ribosomal RNA* and *transfer RNA*, which function in translating the genetic message into *proteins*.

Ribosome, n. (Gr. *soma*, body). Minute particles in the *cytoplasm* of all cells, the site of *protein* synthesis. They consist of protein and **ribosomal RNA.**

Secrete, v. To exude or discharge a substance (secretion), as in a gland.

Selection coefficient. A number giving an estimate of the relative *fitness* of a particular *genotype* in a particular environment.

Speciation, n. The production of new *species*, by splitting or division of ancestral species.

Species (plural species), n. (L. kind). A division of a *genus*; a group of interbreeding natural populations which do not interbreed with other such groups.

Spirochaete, n. (Gr. *speira*, a coil; *chaite*, hair). A type of *bacterium*, flexible and spiral-shaped.

Stabilizing selection. *Natural selection* which tends to maintain the status quo, eliminating deviant or abnormal individuals or *genotypes* from a *species*.

Subspecies, n. A division of a *species*; a group of populations which is geographically defined and whose members differ in some way from other subdivisions of that species.

Substitution mutation. A form of *point mutation* in which one *base-pair* in *DNA* is changed to another.

Symbiosis, n., **symbiotic,** adj. (Gr. *syn*, together; *bios*, life). An association between members of two or more different *species*, to their mutal advantage. The members of the partnership are **symbionts.**

Tectonics, n. (Gr. *tekton*, builder). Structural geology. **Plate tectonics** is the theory that the earth's crust consists of a number of plates which are in motion relative to one another.

Tetraploid. See polyploid.

Transfer RNA. A family of *RNA* molecules, found in the *cytoplasm*, which function in *protein* synthesis by attaching specific *amino acids* to the growing protein *molecule*.

Translocation mutation. Transfer or exchange of parts between non-*homologous chromosomes*.

Triploid. See polyploid.

Vertebrate, n. & adj. An animal with a backbone.

Wild-type, adj. In genetics, the normal or usual condition of an *organism* or a *gene*.

Zygote, n. (Gr. *zygon*, yoke). A fertilized egg; a *diploid* cell produced by fusion of two *haploid gametes*.

Index

Entries in *italics* give the main reference to a topic; entries in **bold** refer to illustrations.